D1258267

# The FBI Story

## Young Readers' Edition

John Edgar Hoover, the Director of the Federal Bureau of Investigation, United States Department of Justice.

# The FBI Story

## Young Readers' Edition

*by* **DON WHITEHEAD**

Foreword by J. Edgar Hoover

RANDOM HOUSE  NEW YORK

© Copyright, 1963, 1956, by Don Whitehead

All rights reserved under International and Pan-American Copyright Conventions. Published in New York by Random House, Inc., and simultaneously in Toronto, Canada, by Random House of Canada, Limited.
Manufactured in the United States of America

Designed by Gertrude Awe and Jean Krulis

Library of Congress catalog card number: 63-17540

***To Boots, Miss Rixon, and my sister,***

***Mrs. J. W. Nolan***

# Foreword

Each year, hundreds of alert-minded students write letters to the FBI, and thousands of others pay visits to our headquarters. We welcome the interest which these young citizens show in our operations. Every American should take a more active role in examining the affairs of his government.

The FBI's record—which is subject to constant review by the courts, the Budget Bureau, committees of Congress, and a corps of vigilant newsmen—speaks clearly for itself.

With the exception of limited areas of the intelligence field where great damage would be done to the national security if full disclosures were made, our day-to-day accomplishments are open to inspection by the public. May this always be true. As long as our country remains free, law enforcement must be responsive to the needs of the people and answerable to them for its actions.

The FBI is a warm, human organization. It is comprised of 14,000 men and women who serve in the 55 field divisions across the United States and Puerto Rico, as well as at Washington headquarters. Some of these employees are recent high school graduates. Others, including alumni of colleges and universities from Maine to California, have been on the rolls for 30 years and more. All pride themselves in meeting the high standards of Fidelity, Bravery and Integrity which are the watchwords of the service.

We are proud of the esprit de corps which exists in the FBI. Ours is a closely knit, "team" organization. Every member has clearly defined duties as well as personal responsibility for the performance of those duties. Investigations are not solved through the efforts of any one person. Our achievements rise from the combined efforts of the organization.

I never miss an opportunity to remind my associates that the FBI was not built into the law enforcement agency it is today by any lone individual. Rather, the combined loyalty and sacrifices of thousands of employees—past and present—were required. We are ever mindful that although one person did not build the FBI, one man can pull it down.

To carry the credentials of the FBI is a heavy responsibility. The Congress, the President and the Attorney General of the United States have entrusted approximately 170 Federal investigative matters to the Bureau's care. These include many of the principal violations of Federal laws.

The FBI investigates criminal acts *only* when there is information indicating that a *Federal* law within its jurisdiction has been violated. My associates and I are constantly alert to the danger of a national police force. We respect the sovereignty of other law enforcement agencies and avoid encroachments upon their authority.

As the investigative arm of the United States Department of Justice, it is the FBI's responsibility to (1) detect violations of Federal laws, (2) locate witnesses and evidence regarding these crimes, and (3) apprehend the persons charged. The facts gathered during our investigations are reported, without recommendation, to the Attorney General and his subordinates for review and decisions as to prosecutive action.

The FBI functions solely as the investigator—not an accuser, prosecutor, jury or judge.

These are among the basic guidelines for the functioning of the FBI which were laid down in the office of the then Attorney General Harlan Fiske Stone at the time I agreed to take over the Bureau's reins. Other points agreed upon were:

> The FBI must be completely divorced from politics.
>
> New appointments to the service were to be based strictly on merit; promotions, on the employee's record and proven ability.
>
> A career service must be established in which vacancies in the higher positions would be filled exclusively from within the ranks.

Chief Justice Stone gave his unqualified support to each of these provisions. And I am happy to acknowledge that they have also received the full endorsement of each of the 12 Attorney Generals since.

The FBI is not a policy-making agency. It is our duty to carry out the policies laid down by others. We do not issue "clearances," attempt to influence administrative decisions, or otherwise interfere in the legitimate affairs of others.

During my lifetime, I have seen sweeping improvements within the law enforcement profession. None of these has been more important than the rapid growth of mutual cooperation. Each month, thousands of requests for the cost-free services of the FBI Laboratory, the Identification Division, and our police training instructors are received from local, county and state agencies. We are glad to comply with as many as possible. These services not only strengthen the bonds of mutual assistance and understanding throughout our profession, but also help to promote greater efficiency, public service and protection of civil rights.

Today, we stand at the threshold of a major breakthrough against crime. All that remains needed are additional public interest and support. These are essential if our country is to forge ahead.

Forge ahead we must, for the odds become more ominous every day. Last year, 70 per cent more serious crimes were committed in the United States than a decade ago. In the past five years, crime has increased nearly four times as fast as our growing population.

Accompanying this crime problem is the deadly threat of subversive enemies of freedom. In 1939, as war clouds rumbled over Europe and Asia, President Franklin D. Roosevelt named the FBI the civilian investigative agency primarily responsible for safeguarding America's internal security. Since that time, our investigations of espionage, sabotage and subversion have increased greatly.

Today, the primary subversive threat is communism—a godless international conspiracy which controls more than one third of the earth's people and a fourth of her land surface. It is represented in this country by a cunning and defiant Communist Party, USA.

One of the Party's foremost goals in America today is to capture the minds of youth. In furtherance of this objective, "front groups" have been formed, special publications issued, and Party spokesmen have embarked on an intensive speech-making campaign at colleges and universities from coast to coast.

There is a great opportunity in law enforcement for outstanding young men and women who wish to devote their lives to the honest and impartial administration of justice. Each year, the FBI receives many more applications for appointments than there are positions to fill. Nonetheless, we invariably are able to find openings for those truly qualified and sincere.

My associates and I are deeply honored that an author of Don Whitehead's outstanding ability and international reputation has taken time to closely study the inner workings of the FBI and prepare this factual report for youth.

Director

# Contents

# The FBI Story
## Young Readers' Edition

# 1. A Mystery at Turkey Creek

The kidnaper who also was a killer planned his crime well—but not well enough to cover his trail which the FBI followed from California across the United States into Canada.

The killer was a quiet, harmless-looking man who liked to be alone. When he came to Denver, Colorado, in December, 1955, the few who became his friends had no way of knowing he had escaped from a prison in California where he was serving time for murder. Neither could they know that the name he used was not his own.

He called himself Walter Osborne. He was 31 years old, a little more than six feet tall and weighed about 170 pounds. He had brown hair, light gray eyes, and glasses to improve the vision in his 20/100 eyes.

When not working at the mixing vats at the Benjamin Moore Paint Co. in Denver, he likely could be found in his apartment reading books on philosophy, adventure, and mysteries. Or else he would head for the nearby mountains to hunt, to fish or merely to roam in the hills. Often he was seen on the mountain trails, ambling along stoop-shouldered and loose-jointed. He never had a companion to share these pleasures. He walked the hills alone.

Perhaps it was on one of these trips into the mountains that he began planning to kidnap Adolph Coors III, a wealthy Colorado businessman, and to demand $500,000 in ransom. No one knows. But when he carried out his plot, he set off one of the greatest manhunts in the long history of the FBI.

He covered his movements carefully before and after the crime. He might even have succeeded in leaving behind a never-to-be-solved mystery had it not been for the remarkable memory of a miner who recalled a fragment of an automobile license number . . . had a truck driver not gone target shooting on a Sunday afternoon . . . and had the FBI not been developed into a scientific crime-fighting organization.

This story began a few minutes before 8 A.M. on February 9, 1960, when 45-year-old Adolph "Ad" Coors said good-by to his wife and four children at their large, comfortable home in the shadows of the Rockies near Morrison, Colorado, west of Denver.

As usual, Coors climbed into his white and blue-green International Travelall station wagon and began the 12-mile drive to the town of Golden. There he and his brothers, Joseph and William, directed the affairs of the two prosperous family businesses, porcelain-making and brewing.

Patches of snow clung to the winter-gray lower slopes of the mountains and Coors was warmly dressed. He wore a tan baseball cap, a navy blue, quilt-lined zipper jacket, dark gray flannel trousers, a white shirt with faint green checks, and a dark tie. A silver tie clasp in the shape of a ski bore his initials, AC III.

Coors drove along a little-traveled road which curved to the northeast, passed over a small stream called Turkey Creek, and entered Soda Lake Road leading to Morrison and Golden. It was at Turkey Creek bridge—only two miles from his home—that Adolph Coors III vanished.

Approximately two hours after Coors left his home, milkman Daniel M. Crocker reached the Turkey Creek bridge on his delivery rounds and found the road blocked by a white and blue-green station wagon.

"Darned careless drivers!" he muttered. He honked the horn of his truck impatiently until he noticed there was no driver behind the wheel of the station wagon. He stepped from his truck and walked across the bridge. The car's engine was running and from the radio came the sound of music.

Crocker returned to his truck and blew the horn for a couple of minutes in short, angry blasts. There was only silence when the echoes of the horn died away.

"I can't wait here all day," Crocker said to himself. He walked back across the bridge. This time he noticed a dark, reddish stain on the bridge floor. It looked like blood. Then, glancing over the side of the bridge, he saw a tan cap and a brown hat lying at the edge of Turkey Creek.

Crocker slid behind the wheel of the station wagon and backed it away from the bridge. He parked it beside the road, switching off the ignition, and continued his deliveries. A short time later, he reached a filling station near Morrison and telephoned the Colorado State Patrol at Golden.

About 11:30 A.M., State Patrolman George Hedricks arrived at Turkey Creek to investigate Crocker's call. He found a card attached to the steering column of the station wagon showing it was registered to the Adolph Coors Company. Hedricks called the Patrol dispatcher on his car radio. "Verify the ownership of this vehicle," he said, describing the Coors car. "See if the Coors company knows anything about it."

Even before the call came from the State Patrol, William and Joseph Coors had been uneasy about the failure of their brother to show up for their weekly executive meeting. They had learned from their sister-in-law that Adolph had left home about 8 A.M. and he had planned to go directly to the office in Golden. It wasn't like him to miss a meeting without telephoning an explanation—but perhaps he had been delayed on an errand and couldn't get to a telephone.

The report of the abandoned car sent the Coors brothers hurrying to Turkey Creek where they and Patrolman Hedricks soon were joined by investigators from the county sheriff's office. The tan cap lying at the water's edge was identified as the one Ad Coors had worn when he left home that morning. The felt hat nearby—a size 7⅜ dark brown fedora—carried the label of the May D & F Company, a Denver store. It had no marks to identify its owner.

Lying in shallow water at the edge of the bridge, a pair of glasses was found by an officer. They were Coors'.

"Ad wouldn't run off and leave his glasses," someone said. "He couldn't see fifteen feet without them."

"It looks pretty bad," another said.

No one seriously considered the possibility that Coors, for some reason of his own, had run away or that he had been attacked by an enemy with a grudge against him.

"Ad Coors didn't have an enemy in this world," one of his close friends said, and everyone else who knew him agreed. There was little if any doubt that he had been kidnaped.

Bridge at Turkey Creek where car belonging to Adolph Coors III was found.

Within a short time, searching parties were fanning out across the rough countryside by horse, by jeep, and by helicopter. But no trace of the missing man was to be found.

At 4:50 P.M., Undersheriff B. Lewis Hawley called the FBI Field Office in Denver and reported the search that was underway for Coors. "We haven't found a sign of him," Hawley said. "It looks as if he has been kidnaped and we may need your help."

Two FBI agents left Denver immediately to relay reports from the Jefferson County sheriff's office in Golden. At this point, there was no evidence of any violation of a federal law but the FBI was prepared to give what help it could. If Coors were missing for 24 hours, it could be presumed he had been kidnaped and forced across a state line. Then the FBI could join in the search under the federal kidnaping statute.

The Denver office at 5:54 P.M. sent a brief summary of the situation by teletype to the FBI headquarters in Washington, D. C. The message ended: "No demands for ransom or otherwise have been received by family. Liaison is being maintained with Jefferson County sheriff's office and Bureau will be advised of any pertinent developments."

After reading this teletype message in Washington, FBI Director J. Edgar Hoover issued an order: "Give top priority to all angles."

That night a list was made of special agents, experienced in criminal investigations of this type, who could be sent to Denver. When no trace of Coors had been found the next morning, a task force of twenty-five agents was ordered to Denver to aid the agents already on the scene. Special Agent in Charge Donald S. Hostetter hurried from his office in Detroit to direct the investigation.

As the agents were pouring into Denver on February 10 by plane and by automobile, Mrs. Adolph Coors III—already in a state of shock—received in the mail the cruelest note of her life. It was a ransom demand, typed on a good quality of bond paper, which said:

> Your husband has been kidnaped. His car is by Turkey Creek.
>
> Call the police or F.B.I.: he dies.
>
> Cooperate: he lives.
>
> Ransom: $200,000 in tens and $300,000 in twenties.
>
> There will be no negotiating . . .
>
> When all set, advertise a tractor for sale in Denver Post section 69. Sign ad King Ranch, Fort Lupton . . . Wait for instructions after ad appears.
>
> Understand this: Adolph's life is in your hands. We have no desire to commit murder. All we want is that money. If you follow the instructions, he will be released unharmed within 48 hours after the money is received.

The Coors family followed the kidnaper's instructions. A want ad was inserted in the Denver Post which read: "John Deere, 1957 model 820, 69 H. P. Tractor for sale—King Ranch, Fort Lupton, Colorado."

Then the family began the nerve-wracking wait as the story of Coors' disappearance leaked out to the press. It was impossible to hide such a story with scores of men scouring the countryside. Headlines bannered the news and, as usual in such cases, brought a flood of false tips from people trying to be helpful.

One by one, the false leads and rumors were run down by the agents. Possible suspects were traced as far as Mexico and Binghamton, N. Y., before their names were dropped from the list.

Then the FBI picked up the first faint trail of the kidnaper. Experts in the Bureau's laboratory in Washington, D. C., found that the ransom note probably had been written on a Royalite portable typewriter. The type-face on the note was identical to that used on this particular portable machine. The paper used by the kidnaper was identified as a watermarked paper known in the trade as "Eaton's Diamond White Bond Berkshire."

With this information, agents began checking Denver stores which sold typewriters and stationery. They found that the May D & F Company—whose name was imprinted in the hat found near the Turkey Creek bridge—also sold Royalite portable typewriters and the same brand of stationery used by the kidnaper.

The store manager turned over the names of everyone who had purchased a Royalite typewriter for months prior to Coors' disappearance. One after another, the names of some 500 people were eliminated as possible suspects until there was only one name remaining—that of a man named William Chiffins.

Store records showed that on October 8, 1959—exactly four months before the kidnaping—a man who called himself William Chiffins had paid $66.55 in cash for one of the machines. He gave his address as 1735 Pennsylvania Street. But when agents made inquiries they found no one at this address or in the neighborhood who had ever heard of Chiffins.

Jerry Davis, the clerk who had sold the typewriter, was questioned. "Could you possibly describe the man who

**An examiner in the document section of the FBI Laboratory, Washington, D. C., compares an extortion letter against the anonymous letter file.**

bought the machine?" an agent asked.

Davis studied the sales slip and then nodded. "I remember him," he said, "because not many customers ever pay cash. He was thirty-five to forty-five, I'd say. Tall fellow. About six feet. He was wearing glasses, the kind that have a plastic frame on top and a metal rim on the lower part. I don't believe he was wearing a hat."

This information, standing alone, was of no use in locating the hunted man or in solving the mystery at Turkey Creek bridge. But it was a teasing clue to be filed away.

Other agents, working with local and state officers, had been questioning everyone who lived near the Coors' home and the bridge, as well as the miners who worked in nearby small ore mines.

Mrs. Pauline Moore, who lived a little more than two miles from the Turkey Creek bridge, said she was hanging her wash on a back-yard line on the morning of February 9 and she distinctly heard a shot in the distance.

"It was so windy I was having trouble hanging the clothes," she said. "I heard a gunshot and I'm sure it came from the direction of Turkey Creek."

Mrs. Rosemary Stitt, who lived about a quarter of a mile from the bridge, told agents she had just finished getting the children off to school when, about 8 o'clock that morning, she heard a sound "like lightning striking a tree." This was approximately the time that Coors would have reached the bridge.

Time after time, agents asked residents in the area if they had noticed any strange automobiles in recent weeks. The agents were told of a 1954 or 1955 Ford sedan, a two-tone Buick, a dark green car that "probably was a Dodge," and a green Ford station wagon. However, the car named most often was a yellow Mercury sedan.

James N. Massey, a cattle breeder, recalled seeing a 1951-model yellow Mercury near the Turkey Creek bridge on four different days prior to Coors' disappearance. "The first three times I saw it," he said, "it was parked facing north into a cave about one hundred yards west of the bridge. I saw it again on the morning of February 8—the day before Ad Coors' car was found. A heavy-shouldered man was sitting behind the wheel. He was wearing a dark brown hat and glasses."

James Roy Cable, a miner who lived nearby, also recalled seeing a yellow Mercury near the bridge on the morning of February 8.

"There has been so much vandalism going on around here that I generally take a good look at any strange car," he said. "This one was a yellow Mercury, all right, with a Colorado license."

"Can you remember the license number?" an agent asked.

Cable said: "I can't say for sure, but I think the license number started with AT 62. It might have been AT 6205 or something like that."

Agents began checking Colorado automobile registrations. The search showed four licenses issued for Mercurys in the AT 6200 series. Among the four was a yellow sedan, sold by a used car dealer in Denver on January 8, 1960, to a Walter Osborne of 1435 Pearl Street.

The address was a three-story apartment building. Agents asked the apartment manager if he had ever had a tenant named Walter Osborne.

"Sure," he said. "Walter Osborne used to live here but he moved out about three weeks ago—on February 10, to be exact. He didn't give any notice. He just knocked on my door about 7:30 in the morning and said he was leaving."

"Did he leave a forwarding address or say where he was going?" an agent asked.

"He said something about going back to Boulder and returning to school," the manager said. "He didn't leave any address."

Had he ever seen Osborne driving a yellow Mercury sedan?

"No," the manager said. "I never saw

a yellow Mercury. He had a gray-and-white Ford which he kept parked in a space right beside the building. He must have sold the car late last December. As far as I know, he didn't buy another one."

Former neighbors of Osborne's described him as a quiet man who kept to himself. Some of them even referred to him jokingly as "the mystery man." He usually wore khaki work clothes which were neat and clean. He spent quite a bit of time washing and polishing his automobile. They had seen him with two or more kinds of guns. This was all they knew of him. None recalled seeing a yellow Mercury.

As these questions were being asked, other agents were looking over the records of law enforcement agencies throughout the area. They found that on January 25, two weeks before Coors' disappearance, an officer had issued a traffic ticket to a Walter Osborne near Morrison, Colorado. He was driving a yellow 1951 Mercury sedan. It was the same car purchased by a Walter Osborne from the Denver used car dealer.

Now things were moving fast. The production manager of the paint company where Osborne had worked remembered him well.

"He was on the 3:30 to 11:30 P.M. shift," he said. "He worked for us for about three and a half years, then he resigned last October. He said he was going back to school. He wasn't absent or late for work a single time. He had a good background—two years of college as well as previous experience with a paint company in Spokane, Washington."

"May we see Osborne's personnel file?" an agent asked.

"Certainly," the manager said. But after looking for the file he said: "It isn't here. Somebody has taken everything out of Osborne's file."

"Were the files kept where Osborne could get to them?"

The manager nodded. "Yes, they were. He could have gotten to them at night when no one was in the office."

Officials at the University of Colorado in Boulder, Denver University, and the Colorado School of Mines all reported they had no record of a student named Walter Osborne. Paint companies in Spokane said they knew nothing of a former worker by that name.

When the name Walter Osborne was relayed to other FBI offices, it brought quick results. On March 4 in Los Angeles, FBI agents found that a man with the same name had worked for an ice company during the Fall of 1955. His description was the same as that of the Osborne wanted in Denver. Company records showed he had joined a union and his dues had entitled him to a life insurance policy. As beneficiary, he had listed the name of Joseph Corbett, Sr., of Seattle, Washington, identified only as "a friend." This information was quickly relayed to Seattle.

Inquiries made in Seattle disclosed that Joseph Corbett, Sr., had a son, Joseph Corbett, Jr., whose description fitted exactly that of Walter Osborne. The son was 31 years old, a little more than six feet tall and weighed about 170 pounds. He wore glasses.

Criminal files showed Joseph Corbett, Jr., had been convicted in California of killing Air Force Sergeant A. L. Reed in December, 1950. The sergeant was found dead, lying on a road on the outskirts of Larkspur, California, with two bullet holes in his head. Los Angeles police had arrested Corbett two weeks later as he was stepping into a stolen car. He was armed with two revolvers, both loaded.

Corbett claimed he picked up Reed, who was hitchhiking. They got into an argument. Reed lunged for a gun on the back seat of the car and he shot him. Corbett pleaded guilty to second degree murder and was sent to San Quentin to serve a ten-year sentence. Early in 1955 he was transferred from San Quentin to the California Institution for Men at Chino. He escaped from Chino in August of that year by removing a screen from a barracks window. It appeared he had obtained a job with the ice company in Los Angeles soon after his escape, and then had made his way to Denver.

Piece by piece, the puzzle fell into place. Agents in Denver got a copy of Walter Osborne's right index fingerprint which had been taken when he applied for a driver's license in 1956 and 1959. The copy was sent to the Bureau in Washington, D. C. Experts in the FBI's Identification Division compared the fingerprint of Walter Osborne with the fingerprint record of Joseph Corbett, Jr., the convicted killer.

The comparison left no doubt. Walter Osborne and Joseph Corbett, Jr. were the same man. Jerry Davis, the department store clerk, was shown a picture of Corbett. "That looks like the man who bought the typewriter," he said.

And so on March 7, 1960—twenty-seven days after Coors vanished at the Turkey Creek bridge—the FBI sent a special airmail notice to all its offices to be on the lookout for Corbett as "a prime suspect" in the Coors abduction. The notices carried a description of Corbett and the yellow Mercury sedan which he had been driving.

Seven days after the wanted notice was circulated, the search for the yellow Mercury ended. An agent in New Jersey found the burned-out hulk of the car near the city dump outside Atlantic City, almost 1,800 miles from Turkey Creek. Witnesses were found who remembered seeing the car burning on the night of February 17, eight days after Coors' disappearance.

On March 30, the FBI added Corbett's name to its list of the "Ten Most Wanted Fugitives." The list went to newspapers, magazines, and police agencies throughout the United States with pictures and a description of the hunted man. Reports came from scores of towns and cities that Corbett had been seen at a restaurant, at a filling station, a movie house, or bus station. But none produced results and the search went on.

As spring came the fate of Coors was still a mystery. Heavy snows and bitter cold, icing over the landscape, had made further searches in the mountains almost impossible. Mrs. Coors had received no further word from the kidnaper after placing the want ad in the Denver *Post*. There had been clumsy attempts by would-be extortionists to obtain money from the Coors family. Each of the notes and calls was recognized as the work of vultures preying on a family's misery. The certainty grew that Coors was dead.

The first solid evidence of what had happened to Coors came on Sunday, September 11, seven months and two days after the kidnaping at Turkey Creek. On that day, 30-year-old Edward Lee Greene, a truck driver, wandered

A fingerprint expert is shown verifying an identification in the assembly section of the FBI Identification Division, Washington, D. C.

**Joseph Corbett, Jr.**

in the hills some 20 miles south of Turkey Creek looking for a spot where he could do some target shooting with his .25 caliber pistol.

He passed a rubbish dump near the road and walked down a steep slope through a stand of pines and aspens. He noticed a pair of brown shoes with spider webs in them, and then he saw a pair of dark gray flannel trousers, badly ripped. He kicked the trousers and heard something jingle.

Curious, Greene picked up the trousers and reached into a pocket. He pulled out 43 cents in change and a set of keys with a silver penknife attached to a short chain. The knife had the initials "AC III" engraved on it.

Later Greene said: "Well, I knew then what it was. It gave me a creepy sort of a feeling and I guess the hair stood up on the back of my head."

Quickly, he scrambled up the slope to his parked car and started for his home in Englewood. Along the way he stopped at the home of C. R. Riddle, an Englewood policeman, and showed him the knife and the keys. Riddle called the FBI and passed along the information.

Greene led FBI agents to the spot where he had stumbled onto the shoes and trousers. Near a bubbling, weed-covered creek the agents found a leather glove and a wrist watch which had belonged to Coors. At intervals down the slope they found his initialed tie clasp, a monogrammed handkerchief, a battered blue nylon jacket, and shirt and undershirt. It appeared the clothing had been ripped from the body of the victim by wild animals dragging it down the slope.

For four days, searchers combed the area. They found a shoulder blade bone which had two holes in it about the size of a .38 caliber bullet—holes which were in direct alignment with holes found in parts of the jacket, shirt and undershirt.

Also, they found a human skull in the underbrush. Mr. Coors' dentist examined the teeth, and after careful comparison with dental records in his office, he identified the skull as positively that of Adolph Coors.

Now the picture was clear enough. The kidnaper had waited for Coors at

Turkey Creek bridge. He had forced him or tricked him into stopping his station wagon. But Coors had not given up meekly. Perhaps he had charged straight at the man holding the pistol, losing his cap and glasses and knocking the kidnaper's hat from his head. A shot had felled Coors—the shot heard by the woman that morning.

With Coors dead or dying, the kidnaper had carried his victim up the mountain road in the yellow Mercury and thrown the body down the mountain slope. Perhaps he fired another bullet into Coors' back to make certain he would never talk. And then he had fled.

The grim hunt for Corbett went on. In October *The Reader's Digest* carried a brief story of the Coors kidnaping along with a picture of Corbett. It was titled "The FBI Wants This Man." The story ended: "Somebody, somewhere, knows this man. If you do, call the FBI at once."

On October 25, a former warehouse worker in Toronto, Canada, was leafing through the *Digest* when the picture of Corbett caught his attention. He read the story and then hurried to the telephone to call the Toronto police. He called their attention to the *Digest* article. "I worked with this fellow during the summer at a warehouse," he said. "He called himself Michael Brent."

This information was relayed by Toronto police to FBI agents. That night a quick check disclosed that Michael Dean Brent—also using the name Walter Osborne—had lived in Toronto from late February to the end of August. He had disappeared from his small apartment, leaving no address.

The next day, a woman who ran a rooming house in Winnipeg also called the police after reading the *Digest* story. She said Corbett had once roomed at her place.

Agents quickly picked up Corbett's trail. Working closely with the Canadian police, they found he had used the names Michael MacLean and Ian N. McIntosh while living in Winnipeg from September 3 until October 8. Then he rented a fire-engine-red Pontiac and disappeared. Descriptions of the red Pontiac and Corbett were furnished to police stations across Canada.

In Vancouver, British Columbia, a police officer pondered the description and recalled he had seen a bright red Pontiac drive into a motor hotel about two weeks earlier. Immediately checking at the hotel, he learned that the driver of the Pontiac was still registered there under the name Thomas Wainwright.

Within minutes, a squad of Vancouver police officers and FBI agents were guarding the hotel's exits. Then an officer knocked on the door of the room occupied by Wainwright.

When the door opened, Joseph Corbett, Jr., stood looking at the armed men in the hallway for a moment. Then he said meekly: "I give up. I'm the man you want. I'm not armed." A loaded automatic pistol was found in a zipper bag near the bed.

The FBI returned Corbett to Colorado where state authorities charged him with the murder of Adolph Coors III. He was not tried in a federal court because the federal kidnaping law had not been broken since Coors had not been carried into another state.

Corbett sullenly refused to talk. But the evidence against him, collected by the FBI, was so convincing that a jury convicted him of murder on March 29, 1961. He was sentenced to life imprisonment, with no hope of parole.

The kidnap-murder of Adolph Coors III is only one of uncounted thousands of cases solved by the agents of the Federal Bureau of Investigation. But the telling of the story gives a glimpse into how the FBI operates today through agents who are experts in the field of law enforcement.

# 2. 2,000 Miles of Danger

The FBI is now more than fifty years old. It is known around the world for its efforts to make efficiency and honesty an everyday practice in police work and not something that is unusual. Yet until recently it remained a sort of mystery organization, with few people knowing how it operated in fighting criminals, protecting civil rights and guarding against espionage.

There is, of course, nothing mysterious about the FBI. It is simply a highly trained force of men who work under stern rules of discipline, laid down by Director J. Edgar Hoover, in a never-ending struggle against criminals and subversives. The Congress, the Attorney General, and the President of the United States decide which laws and directives are to be enforced by the FBI, and once the laws are passed the FBI shoulders the burden.

Discipline within the FBI is as strict as that of the U. S. Marine Corps. Hoover has insisted there must never be a scandal connected with the Bureau because: "One man didn't build the FBI, but one man can tear it down."

The life of an FBI agent isn't an easy one. He must follow the rules—rules which may seem inconsequential until they help save lives in emergency situations. He must be ready to leave home at a moment's notice on dangerous missions anywhere in the country. He must keep himself physically fit and become an expert at self-defense and the use of firearms. He must be ready to work long hours while trailing a suspected criminal or spy, or while searching records, files and columns of figures for one small clue. He learns quickly that a small piece of information, even a bit of dirt on a shoe, might prove to be the key to solving a case.

He can not drink whiskey while on a case. He is forbidden to use force or strongarm methods in getting information from suspects. He can not accept rewards or gifts for doing his duty. He must pay his taxes and other legal debts. But these are merely a few of the rules of conduct which guide the agents in their work.

**FBI Laboratory examiner compares the photograph of a heel print with the heel of a suspect's shoe.**

The reason for these rules is that the FBI was not always an organization that was worthy of respect. In its early years many of its agents were chosen because they had powerful friends in politics and not because they were men of ability. The methods used in investigations often were worse than the crimes that had been committed.

All this has changed. The change within the FBI began in 1924 when Herbert Hoover (who later became President of the United States) suggested to Attorney General Harlan Fiske Stone that 29-year-old J. Edgar Hoover be given the task of rebuilding the FBI. Young Hoover was no relation to the man who was to be President.

Hoover was named FBI Director and he started out by bringing together college-trained men who would be guided by the rule that proving one man's innocence was just as important as producing evidence to prove another man's guilt.

Hoover put together a hard-hitting force of young agents who were willing and able to move into roaring gun battles against the gangsters. For years the mobs terrorized the country much as the bad men of the Old West terrorized frontier towns—with guns and violence.

Out of this force grew the modern FBI, a highly trained corps of 6,000 special agents backed by 8,000 technicians, specialists, stenographers, and clerks stationed in the Washington, D. C., headquarters and fifty-five field divisions across the country.

The FBI has men who are specially trained to combat Communist efforts to obtain military secrets and to undermine the government of the United States. But the greater part of the FBI manpower through the years has been used to fight a rising rate of crime, mostly in the big cities.

It is not unusual for Hoover to move as many as fifty men into a single investigation such as the Coors kidnaping. Nor is it unusual for the FBI to mobilize more than a hundred men when the lives of many people are endangered by a madman—or even a fool.

Such a case developed a few years ago in California when a man desperately in need of money threatened to blow up Sunset Limited Train No. 2 unless he received $500,000 from the Southern Pacific Railroad. The mailing of the note demanding the money was itself a violation of the Federal Extortion Act—and nearly 150 agents across five states went into action to prevent the unknown man from carrying out his threat.

This story began on May 16, 1958, when James H. Pruett, Jr., a Southern Pacific Railroad manager, opened his mail and found a crudely typed letter which said:

**MAT—ER OF LIFE OR DEATH**
**READ VERY VERY CAREFULLY**

It is very important that every step of this program go exactly as it is written here.

1. If one thing you are instructed to do is not kept in complete secret any one of your passenger trains that run on the west coast will be blown off the track with dynamite . . .

2. What you are to do.

Put 500,000 dollars in 20 dollar bills only firmly packed in an unlocked box that will not break open by hard fall. Put box in mail bag which is well secured. Put mail bag containing the box

FBI agent in quick draw series.

of money on the SUNSET LIMITED NO. 2 May 23, 1958. Instruct a member of the crew who can see the roadway clearly at all times to throw the bag off the train as close as possible where he sees a strange flashing light. The train is to proceed on as usual . . . I don't think 500,000 dollars means so much to a railroad co. as to be so foolish as to sacrifice a train load of pass. . . . The saftey of your pass. from this monent on depends on how well you can read and beleive it. That is all.

Company officials decided this was a case that should be handled by the FBI. While the threat might have been made by a harmless crank, no chances could be taken with the lives of so many people by ignoring it. The note was turned over to Ralph W. Bachman, assistant special agent in charge of the Los Angeles FBI office.

The FBI had less than one week in which to capture the mystery man—this Mr. X who had set May 23 as the deadline for delivery of the money. If he were not caught in time, then a train loaded with passengers might be "blown off the track some place somewhere in the night . . ." And the FBI also had to consider the possibility that other persons might be assisting Mr. X in this extortion plot.

But where was the most likely place for this Mr. X to be waiting for the money? The note gave no hint where he would be with the flashing light. It could be anywhere along the 2,000-mile route of the Sunset Limited No. 2, stretching from Los Angeles to New Orleans.

Each night this train rolled out of the Los Angeles Union Station at 9:25 (8:25, Pacific Standard Time). It moved slowly at first through a maze of railroad yard tracks, across highways and streets, and then picked up speed for the run to Palm Springs. Leaving this desert resort, the train then moved through the mountains and into the vast desert of the Southwest. It passed through Yuma, Arizona, near the Mexican border, and then sped on to Phoenix and Tucson. It passed through Lordsburg, New Mexico, and paused at El Paso, Texas. From El Paso, it carried its passengers on to San Antonio and Houston and then to their final destination in New Orleans.

At some places the railroad ran side by side with the highways. But there were long, lonely stretches of track in the desert which were as much as forty miles from the nearest highway.

Working closely with officers of the Southern Pacific, FBI Agent Bachman and his aides worked out a plan by which agents could keep a watch over the train along every mile of its 2,000-mile route.

First, the plan called for agents to be stationed in the cab of the locomotive and in the last car of the train. Other agents would be placed at street and highway intersections and at points where the tracks ran near a highway. Agents in automobiles would be stationed at points along the highways to look for any unusual flashing signals. When the train left one FBI Field Office zone and entered another, fresh teams of agents would take over.

On those long desert stretches far from the highways, the train was to be watched over by agents in Air Force and Coast Guard helicopters which these services had promised to supply.

All the agents were to be equipped with radios. An automobile with a two-way radio was to be stationed at a mountain-top pass near Los Angeles. It would act as a relay point for messages sent from the Control Center in Los Angeles and the mobile units along the train's route.

The plan was approved by FBI headquarters, and on May 20 Director Hoover sent a message to the Los Angeles office saying: "This investigation is to be vigorously pursued . . . Every effort must be expended to identify and locate subject . . . Keep Bureau promptly advised of all developments. . . ."

The next day an urgent teletype message was sent from Los Angeles to FBI Field Offices in Phoenix, Albuquerque, El Paso, San Antonio, Houston and New Orleans. It said:

> . . . Sunset Limited leaves Los Angeles 8:25 P.M., Pacific Standard Time, May 23 next. Twenty-five watt FM radio transmitter and aerial being installed on main locomotive. Two agents and Road Foreman of Engineers will ride in cab. Two additional agents will ride in rear car for observation . . . Two agents to ride in plane and maintain radio contact with train and ground units. From Pomona, cars strategically placed along highway paralleling railroad to Yuma will maintain radio contact with train. Phoenix, Albuquerque, El Paso, San Antonio, Houston and New Orleans consult Sunset Limited timetable and arrange similar automobile radio coverage from Yuma to New Orleans by arrangement with offices in adjoining territory. Locomotive changes in San Antonio; therefore San Antonio arrange for installation of antenna on cab and use of transmitter for radio contact from San Antonio to New Orleans . . . In order to afford continuity, two Los Angeles agents will ride train from Los Angeles to New Orleans. Phoenix have two agents board train at Phoenix to relieve other two Los Angeles agents. El Paso board two agents to relieve Phoenix agents. San Antonio board two agents to relieve El Paso agents and continue to New Orleans . . . Establish liaison with Southern Pacific Railroad special agents who are being alerted . . . All offices advise the Bureau and Los Angeles by teletype by noon, Pacific Standard Time, May 23 next, details of coverage established.

Now the plan was set. Two metal boxes were fashioned in the railroad's shop in Los Angeles and two heavy canvas sacks were borrowed from the post office. Twin packages were prepared just in case those aboard the train should mistake a railroad signal light for the flashing light of Mr. X and toss out a package at the wrong place. The boxes were stuffed with paper.

In a conference with railroad officials, Bachman said: "If the writer of the letter should call, try to find out where we can expect his signal, and exactly what kind of signal it will be. If we can narrow this down to one stretch of track, it will simplify things for all of us."

At noon on May 23, the FBI offices along the route of the Sunset Limited reported they were ready. And then at 3:15 P.M. the telephone rang in the Southern Pacific office of Lloyd V. Greer, secretary to Manager James H. Pruett, Jr. A man's voice asked to speak to Pruett.

"I'm sorry," Greer said, "but Mr. Pruett is out of his office. He is arranging for a meeting he has tonight."

"Do you know if Pruett received a

letter about a week ago?" the caller asked. "Is the meeting tonight about this letter?"

"That's right," Greer replied. "But listen. Mr. Pruett is afraid he might miss your signal. He's concerned about how long he is going to have to ride the train. In other words, he isn't sure just what type of signal to look for. Will it be a flashing signal? Will it be waved from side to side, up or down, or will it be a flashing red light, like a brakeman's lantern?"

Mr. X said: "Yes, that's it. Like a brakeman's lantern."

Greer said: "Can you tell us whether or not to expect the signal on this side of Beaumont Pass or on the other side?"

"I don't know," Mr. X said. "I'll call back at 4:30. I am going to have a hard time getting this information to them."

"You probably have to tell several people?"

"That's right," the man said, and hung up.

At 4:30 P.M. Mr. X again called Greer's office. Part of the conversation went like this:

Mr. X: "Is it all right?"

Greer: "Mr. Pruett seemed to think so. There are a couple of details he wanted answered. He asked again if you could give us any idea at all where he could expect to put the thing off."

Mr. X: "I don't think it will be too far but I don't know at this time. That is being arranged by the other party . . . I don't think it will be past Indio. I don't believe so . . ."

Agents tried to trace the calls to their source, but the best they could do was to establish that the calls had been made from pay stations somewhere outside the eastern edge of Los Angeles.

The kind of signal Mr. X would use posed a problem. The railroad rules called for the engineer to bring his train to a halt whenever he saw a red light along the railroad right-of-way. It was decided that the Southern Pacific's division superintendent, Paul D. Robinson, should ride aboard the locomotive with the two FBI agents to identify signal lights, and to take responsibility for passing any strange red light along the route.

A heavy fog hung over Southern California on May 21–22 but the night of Friday, May 23, was clear and mild. Early in the evening Robinson, two FBI agents, and Foreman of Engines Raul C. Hayden climbed aboard the Diesel locomotive in the railroad yards. They concealed themselves in the "nose cone" of the engine so that no one could see them when the train moved through the yards.

Engineer B. O. Bailiff asked no questions since the two strangers were accompanied by railroad officials. In fact, it was not unusual for the company to invite newsmen, magazine writers, and television people to ride in the forward part of the locomotive.

The Sunset Limited No. 2 pulled out of Union Station in Los Angeles at 9:27 P.M., two minutes behind schedule. It was then that Superintendent Robinson disclosed to the locomotive crew the real purpose of their presence. The FBI agents began at once to hook their radio equipment onto the emergency antenna. Within minutes they were in touch with the two agents in the rear car of the train and with the entire emergency network.

The agents stood with Robinson behind Engineer Bailiff and Fireman V. L.

Roberts. Robinson and Hayden called out the names of the streets, highways, and landmarks as the train passed them. In this way the location of the train was known to every agent listening on the network stretching far into the desert country.

Looking from the window of the locomotive, the agents suddenly were aware of how many lights there were along the tracks of a railroad. Flashing stop lights, red signal lights at crossings and on nearby railroad tracks, flashing red neon lights at filling stations and stores, the headlights and taillights of automobiles and trucks . . . lights by the hundreds. They wondered if anyone possibly could pick out the flashing light of Mr. X somewhere ahead in the darkness.

The Sunset Limited No. 2 paused briefly at the suburb of Alhambra and then picked up speed for the 50-mile run to its next stop, with Engineer Bailiff trying to make up the two minutes lost in leaving Union Station. None of the passengers aboard that night was aware of his role in this strange drama.

As the locomotive rounded a slight curve about nineteen miles east of Los Angeles, rolling along at seventy miles an hour, Robinson saw a red light flashing near the right side of the tracks. He knew it was not a part of the railroad's signal system.

"There it is!" he exclaimed. It was 10:07 P.M.

Quickly, one of the agents shoved a canvas sack out of the window of the locomotive as the train thundered by the light without slowing its pace. At the same time the second agent tossed a glass jar of red paint and a plastic bag filled with "glitter" from the other window to mark the spot.

All this took place in a matter of seconds. During this time one of the agents was talking into a radio microphone: "There's the light! . . . We're going to drop! . . . It's out!"

The voice from the locomotive was picked up by the radio control center and also by two agents whose car was following the train along a side road only a short distance from where the sack had been hurled from the engine. The Control Center ordered the two agents to move out quickly. The rear lights of the Sunset Limited No. 2 had barely faded in the distance before they were on their way to the scene.

Working their way cautiously to the railroad, the agents located the mail sack lying at the bottom of an embankment. Nowhere did they see a flashing light nor could they hear anyone moving about.

The finding of the sack was reported to the Control Center by walkie-talkie radio. "Set up a surveillance," the Control Center ordered. Other agents in the area were told to remain at a distance.

The two agents crawled into a thick patch of weeds, leaving the mail sack where they found it. They lay waiting, listening to the insects and the other voices of the night. For more than an hour they waited, saying nothing.

Near midnight, they heard a slight noise like the sound of tall weeds being rustled apart. Then they saw a shadow moving slowly alongside the tracks. The shadow became the figure of a man creeping on hands and knees. He stopped when he reached the sack and turned it over.

It was then that the agents, guns drawn, leaped from hiding and caught him in the beams of their flashlights.

"Don't move!" an agent commanded. "We are FBI agents."

The man crouched there before them was middle-aged, more than six feet tall, and weighed about 180 pounds. He wore a black-and-red work jacket over a white T-shirt, gray trousers, and black boots. He stared wildly at the agents.

"You've got the wrong man," he stammered.

Within minutes, other agents were on the scene. The man was 35 years old, a frequently jobless truck driver and the father of two sons, aged 10 and 11.

At first he claimed he knew nothing of the extortion note. He said he had met two men in Compton, California, the day before and they had promised to pay him $200 if he would flash a red light at that spot.

But finally the man confessed. "I didn't really mean to blow up that train," he said. "I don't know anything about dynamite. I just thought if I threatened the railroad, they'd throw some money off the train. I didn't expect them to throw off $500,000."

He told of an unhappy life at home, arguments with his wife, the loss of his job, and the wild desire to force someone to give him some money so that he could buy his family the things they wanted—and take them on a vacation. That was when he got the idea of writing the letter to the Southern Pacific. He had found the name and address of Manager Pruett in a travel folder and he had borrowed a typewriter from a neighbor to write the note.

When the Sunset Limited No. 2 passed, he was flashing the light but he didn't see the bag thrown from the window of the locomotive. Uncertain whether the extortion money had been dropped, he had walked with the light to his truck which was parked nearby and had driven around the area looking for police cars or other indications that officers were in the area. Then he had returned to search for the sack—only to be caught.

At one point, he said plaintively: "Gee, fellows, I'd like to say I'm sorry. Can't we forget this thing, let me apologize and go home?"

The attempted extortion could hardly be wiped off the record with an apology. But the court was sympathetic and the man served less than a year in prison.

In this case, the man who threatened the lives of scores of people aboard the Sunset Limited No. 2 may never have carried out his threat. But who knows? The next man may mean every word of his threat—and for that reason the FBI can take no chances.

# 3. Spies and Saboteurs

The FBI was born in a tempest—a dispute between President Theodore Roosevelt and Congress that started soon after Roosevelt entered the White House in September, 1901.

The man who touched off the uproar in the capital was Roosevelt's Secretary of the Interior, Ethan A. Hitchcock of Missouri. After a few months in office, Hitchcock suspected that some government employees and perhaps even a few members of Congress were guilty of what amounted to the theft of government-owned land in the Far West.

Over the years, the federal government had set aside almost forty million Western acres as forest reserves. The land was too rough and broken for farming, but the timber on the land was worth many millions of dollars and some of it was good for cattle grazing.

Hitchcock was told that large tracts were being sold illegally and that some of the Land Office's own people were involved along with others. Quietly, he sent a man to investigate. The reports this man brought back left no doubt the situation was even worse than Hitchcock had thought.

The Secretary asked the Department of Justice to make an investigation even though the Department then had no agent force of its own for gathering evidence—not even if the President himself knew the law was being violated and asked for the facts.

Soon after the Civil War, the Secret Service had been organized to halt a flood of counterfeiting. A bit later Congress also had approved an expanded force of agents for the Customs Service so it could fight the smuggling of goods from overseas. But no investigators had ever been approved for the Justice Department despite the fact that this was the Department responsible for enforcing most of the laws passed by Congress.

Having no agents of its own, the Department "borrowed" agents from the Secret Service and sent them to the Far West to look into the reported thefts of land. The agents found that men were fencing government land and using it as their own. Large tracts were being sold to timber companies and to private owners.

The reports from the Secret Service agents led to the indictment of scores of people. Many were convicted of fraud, including a United States Senator. But the methods used in prosecuting the cases enraged many members of Congress. There was reason for this anger because witnesses had been forced through threats by private detectives to give false testimony and juries had been "rigged" against the defendants in some cases.

In the uproar that followed, a move was made in Congress to forbid the Department of Justice from using Secret Service agents in its investigations. There also were charges that Roosevelt had been using "detectives" to spy on the senators and representatives who opposed him.

Roosevelt fought to block the move. He said it would "work very great damage to the government in its endeavor to prevent and punish crime" and that "there is no more foolish outcry than this against 'spies;' only criminals need fear our detectives." There were other protests, too. But Congress was in no mood to listen. The bill was passed.

Now unable to call for help from the Secret Service, Roosevelt ordered Attorney General Charles J. Bonaparte to organize his own force of agents within the Department of Justice without Congress's approval. Bonaparte issued the order on July 26, 1908, and this was the beginning of the FBI.

In its early years, the agency was called the Bureau of Investigation. It had no training program for its agents. Those who did join were poorly paid and frequently lacked experience in law enforcement. The Bureau chiefs had little real control over the men. They could transfer a man from one city to another—but often these moves were blocked by politicians looking after their friends.

This weak, untrained, undisciplined Bureau was the chief agency on which the United States government had to depend for internal security when the guns of World War I began roaring in Europe in August, 1914.

The German government could not have chosen a better time to send two agents to the United States to set up an espionage and sabotage ring. It was the first such ring to be organized in this country by a foreign power since the Revolutionary War. The two agents were Count Johann von Bernstorff, German ambassador to the United States, and Dr. Heinrich Albert, the German commercial attaché.

They arrived in New York aboard a transatlantic liner in August. Since both of them were in the German diplomatic service, they were given the courtesy of passing through Customs without an inspection of their luggage. Had von Bernstorff's luggage been opened, Customs agents would have found $150,000,000 in German treasury notes—money which was to be used to finance the spying and dynamiting of American defense plants. But no one did open it.

In fact, there were few who thought this country needed protection from spies and saboteurs, or that there was any real danger even though a war was being fought in Europe. Americans felt safe because of the almost 4,000 miles of ocean that separated them from Europe. As a result, the government had never taken the trouble to organize an intelligence service worthy of the name.

When von Bernstorff reached the German embassy in Washington, he quickly set to work to put together his organization. Dr. Albert was responsible for handling the money and business end of the operations; Captain Karl Boy-Ed, the naval attaché, was to arrange for the sabotage of any American ships that might be carrying arms to Great Britain, France, or Russia; and Captain Franz von Papen, the military attaché, was in charge of all other espionage and sabotage.

In January, 1915—five months after von Bernstorff and Dr. Albert arrived in New York and two years before the United States entered the war—the German General Staff sent a secret message to the German embassy in Washington which said:

> For Military Attaché: People fit for sabotage in United States and Canada can be ascertained from the following persons: (three names listed) . . . In United States sabotage can reach to

Karl Boy-Ed.

> all kinds of factories for war deliveries; railroads, dams, bridges must not be touched there. Under no circumstances compromise Embassy . . .

Then came a series of mysterious explosions across the country which blew up ammunition dumps, powder plants, guncotton storehouses and chemical plants. Factories making war materials were gutted by fires. Fires broke out on American ships which were headed for Europe with war supplies.

In the early morning hours of July 30, 1916, two million pounds of dynamite exploded on Black Tom Island in New York harbor. The fearful blast was heard 100 miles away. It shattered windows throughout Jersey City and broke heavy plate glass windows in Manhattan and Brooklyn. Three men and a child were killed. The blast also destroyed the island as an important transfer point for supplies being shipped to Europe.

Six months later, a similar explosion blew up a shell assembly plant in Kingsland, New Jersey, causing $17 million damage.

Not until after the war was the United States to learn the vast extent of Germany's success in destroying vital American facilities. But even when a spy or a saboteur was caught, he could not be charged with espionage or sabotage. There were no federal laws at this time making sabotage or espionage a crime.

One of the most brilliant and successful of the German agents was Franz von Rintelen. He spoke English fluently. He knew America and American ways well because he had once spent several months in this country studying banking.

In the spring of 1915, Berlin sent a message to Ambassador von Bernstorff which said: "Inform Rintelen who arrives today . . . about Papen's proposals." This was followed by a message saying: "Inform Boy-Ed as to Papen's proposals for transmission to Rintelen."

Von Rintelen arrived in the United States, by way of Norway, carrying a forged Swiss passport and posing as a businessman. Actually he was an officer in the German navy and such a trusted agent that he had authority to spend up to $500,000 in carrying out his plots.

The first move von Rintelen made was to organize a company in New York known as E. V. Gibbons, Inc. The firm specialized in finding and exporting war supplies for Germany's enemies. On the surface, the company appeared to be anti-German. But it was a front behind which von Rintelen could obtain the sailing schedules of ships and learn which cargoes were going where. This was valuable information for his agents whose job it was to hide fire-bombs aboard ships. The bombs were timed to explode when the ships were at sea.

The bomb was the invention of a German-born scientist, Dr. Walter T. Scheele, who had lived in the United States for twenty-five years. When the war began, he was eager to do something for his native country. He was recruited into von Bernstorff's ring.

When von Rintelen heard of Scheele's fire-bomb invention, he put the scientist to work in Hoboken turning out from thirty-five to fifty bombs a day. He had no trouble locating men—for a price—who would hide the bombs in the holds of outgoing ships. In this manner it is believed von Rintelen was able to destroy or to damage the cargoes in some thirty-six ships, valued at $10,000,000.

Bureau of Investigation agents got on von Rintelen's trail when he boldly tried to buy 300,000 rifles from the United States government while using an assumed name. A short time later a Secret Service agent was trailing Dr. Albert, who had arrived in New York with von Bernstorff. When Dr. Albert left his brief case unguarded for a moment on the seat of an elevated train, the agent snatched it and ran.

Papers found in the Albert brief case revealed some of the operations of the ring and its link with the German embassy. By this time many millions of dollars of damage had been done by the German agents.

Congress declared war on Germany on April 6, 1917. The final break came over the German submarines' sinking of American ships at sea without warning.

President Woodrow Wilson turned over to the Bureau of Investigation the job of policing the "enemy aliens"—Germans who were not American citizens. At this time the Bureau had only 300 agents, and there were more than 1,000,000 male aliens who were required to register. The agents also were expected to guard against espionage and sabotage, to protect harbors and war factories, to aid in locating army deserters, and then to carry on their regular work of investigating federal law violations.

Even when 100 agents were added to the Bureau rolls the burden was more than the agents could handle. Bureau Chief A. Bruce Bielaski was appalled at the work load. For that reason he became interested in the plan of a Chicago advertising executive, A. M. Briggs.

Briggs proposed that he and other citizens be allowed to organize groups of loyal Americans who would serve without pay in helping the Bureau. This aid would cost the government nothing, Briggs said. The citizens would pay any costs out of their own pockets.

The idea sounded good to both Bielaski and Attorney General Thomas W. Gregory. Encouraged to go ahead, Briggs at once formed what he called the American Protective League (APL), with national headquarters in Chicago.

There rarely has been anything like it in the history of the United States. The APL's membership climbed rapidly to 100,000 and then leaped to 250,000. Units were organized in every major city in the land. For 75 cents, each member received a badge which was to be worn, but concealed. The leaders made it clear that the badge did not give anyone police powers, but all too often, such warnings were soon forgotten.

Secretary of the Treasury William McAdoo was disturbed because the badges carried the words "Secret Service" when in fact the APL had no connection whatever with the government's Secret Service. He wrote to Attorney General Gregory recalling that a volunteer citizens' organization much like the APL had been tried during the Revolutionary War, but it had "committed grave abuses and injustices." He said the APL "contains the same evil potentialities . . ."

McAdoo was right. The APL became a disorganized, undisciplined army of "detectives" in which the good work of a few was lost in the injustices done by many. Men were arrested without cause and searches were made illegally. Labor leaders complained some APL members were interfering in labor-management disputes and taking sides against strikers. Innocent people reported that APL volunteers were high-handedly creating the false impression that they were federal officers.

The urge to "do something to help the country" in time of war spread like a virus. Men sometimes committed violent crimes in the name of patriotism. In Butte, Montana, six masked men entered a boarding house and seized a man who they thought was not as loyal to the United States as he should be. Giving him no chance for a fair trial, they hanged him from a railroad trestle.

This state of affairs caused President Wilson to speak out against "the great danger of citizens taking the law into their own hands." At times when the APL volunteers were called on by the Justice Department to do police work, newspapers charged a "monstrous invasion of human rights" and a "shameful abuse of power."

Out of this mess came the lesson that law enforcement and the guarding of American security are jobs for trained, professional agents—not for amateurs, no matter how well-meaning they might be. The American Protective League was disbanded, never to be reorganized, soon after the war ended on November 11, 1918, with the defeat of Germany.

# 4. New Enemies to Fight

The American soldiers returned home from World War I to the cheers of millions. Celebrations were staged across the land. Prayers of thanksgiving were said for the end of the killing on the battlefields. But the silencing of the guns had not brought peace as most people dreamed that it would.

Around the world there still was unrest, bitterness and revolution. Before the war had ended, the Czar of Russia had stepped down from his throne, his armies in revolt, with soldiers throwing down their rifles and refusing to fight. For a few months Russia was ruled by men seeking to form a government in which there would be free elections and the people at last would have a chance to name their own leaders.

But a small group of Bolsheviki (Communists) headed by Nikolai Lenin fought to gain power for themselves. Their aim was to set up a dictatorship in which they, and not the people, would control Russia. If they could do this, they were certain that revolutions would sweep Communists into power in every country.

The Communists succeeded in Russia. Promising "land and bread" to the peasants—and no more war—they crushed the young government of Russia. Lenin said: "Now we have a revolution. The peasants and workmen control the government. This is only a preliminary step toward a similar revolution everywhere."

The revolution in Russia had its admirers in the United States. They, too, were eager to overthrow the government of the United States and establish a "new order." They announced their aim with a wave of terror.

It came on the night of June 2, 1919. Violent explosions jarred Washington, D. C., Philadelphia, Pittsburgh, New York, Boston, Cleveland, Newtonville, Massachusetts, and Paterson, New Jersey.

In Washington, the night was warm and star-filled. Near midnight, Assistant Secretary of the Navy Franklin D. Roosevelt (later to be President) drove through the quiet streets to his home at No. 2131 R Street and entered his house. About the same time Attorney General A. Mitchell Palmer and his wife snapped off the lights in their first-story library and went to their bedroom upstairs.

The Palmers heard something thump against their front door. Then the house shook from the blast of explosives. Part of the front wall was blown in, wrecking the library where the Palmers had been sitting a few minutes earlier. Windows were blown out of the Roosevelt home across the street and houses were damaged two blocks away. Fortunately, the Palmers were unhurt.

Police rushed to the scene to find bits of clothing and parts of the bodies of two men in the wreckage. Apparently the dynamiters had used a faulty fuse and had been blown up by their own bomb. Scattered about were handbills which read:

**Plain Words**

**The powers that be make no secret of their will to stop here in America the worldwide spread of revolution . . . Class war is on, and cannot cease but with a**

Copyright Underwood & Underwood

**Damaged home of A. Mitchell Palmer, Attorney General, Washington, D. C., June, 1919. This outrage was part of a nation-wide bomb plot.**

**complete victory for the international proletariat . . .**

Only a month earlier bombs had been sent through the mails addressed to well-known men including John D. Rockefeller, banker J. P. Morgan, three members of the President's Cabinet, a Supreme Court justice, four U. S. senators, two U. S. representatives, a U. S. district judge, and two governors. Most of the bombs were intercepted. One exploded, injuring a servant of Senator and Mrs. Thomas W. Hardwick of Georgia.

The terrorism caused a wave of outrage across the nation. It brought demands for the federal government to find and to punish those who had done these things. The Department of Justice set up an intelligence division to make a thorough study of the activities of all groups who were urging force and violence to overthrow the government, as well as to determine what prosecutive action could be taken against them. The man placed in charge of this division was 24-year-old J. Edgar Hoover, then a Special Assistant to the Attorney General.

Hoover dug into the background of those who had been preaching violence. He found they were divided roughly into three groups—the anarchists, the International Workers of the World, and the Communists. The anarchists were opposed to all governments, regardless of their nature. The IWW wanted a state controlled by workers.

As for the Communists, Hoover saw that they were the most dangerous of all. He was convinced by the Communist leaders' own words that each Party member was a willing agent of Moscow, engaged in a plot to place communism in power in every country in the world by force, violence and subversion.

It became clear to him their aim was to destroy the old governments as well as the old religions and the private ownership of property. Factories, farms, houses, apartments, banks—everything—would belong to the state. Children would be taught to be atheists. There would be nothing more important than the Communist state.

It was shortly before Hoover began making this study that Moscow sent to the United States the first official representative from the Soviet Union. He was Ludwig C. A. K. Martens who, it was rumored, had brought $200,000,000 in gold to be used in making trade agreements. His secretary was Santerri Nuorteva who had charge of Communist propaganda in this country.

Martens talked a great deal about making deals for American-made goods, but about all he ever did was to take part in Communist propaganda drives. It soon became clear that Martens was more interested in enlisting recruits for the Reds' cause than in trade.

Bureau agents discovered that a Swedish sailor was acting as a Communist courier, smuggling envelopes to Martens. One envelope was found to contain $50,000 in diamonds to be used for paying the cost of the Reds' propaganda drive in the United States. Martens at last was forced to leave the country.

For a time the Communist Party was driven underground and the members carried on their work in the greatest of secrecy as they tried to win places of power in the nation's labor unions and to enlist new members in their cause. Before many years had passed, they were out again in the open—denying the Party was a tool of Moscow or that it was trying to overthrow the United States government by force and violence.

**Ludwig C. A. K. Martens**

The years that followed World War I were years of unrest. Scandals were uncovered in the administration of President Warren G. Harding. Men of prominence were accused and sent to prison for defrauding the Treasury of millions of dollars. It is hardly surprising that in this period a secret society known as the Ku Klux Klan grew into a powerful organization whose influence reached into forty-six states from Maine to California.

In its written purpose, the Klan was "to protect the weak, the innocent, and the defenseless from the indignities, wrongs and outrages of the lawless, the violent, and the brutal; to relieve the injured and oppressed; to succor the suffering and the unfortunate . . ."

These were noble-sounding aims. Actually, the Klan was anti-Negro, anti-Catholic, and anti-Jew.

The first Klan was born in the terrible days after the Civil War when the South was struggling to rebuild its shattered cities and fortunes. Some say it was started in Pulaski, Tennessee, by a group of young men who formed a club because they were bored—and who found it was amusing to ride around the countryside at night on horseback wearing hoods and frightening people. Then hooded men used the Klan as a means to terrify Negroes and to take the law into their own hands.

The old Klan died out. But in 1915 Colonel William S. Simmons of Atlanta (at least he called himself colonel) revived the Klan with the aid of a shrewd publicity agent named Edward Young Clarke. Each new member paid a $10 initiation fee, of which $8 went to Clarke and $2 went to Simmons. Robes and hoods that cost $1.25 were sold by Simmons and Clarke to the members for $6.50. The Klan membership swelled into tens of thousands.

**Col. William Joseph Simmons, Second Imperial Wizard and Founder of the New Klan. (From *Knights of the Ku Klux Klan* by Col. Winfield Jones, Copyright 1941.)**

There were towns where the Klan operated merely as a fraternal lodge or as a political club. But in other places hooded men began to terrorize families, then towns and sometimes an entire state.

In September, 1922, J. Edgar Hoover —then an assistant director in the Bureau of Investigation—listened to a strange tale told by Paul Wooton, Washington correspondent for the New Orleans *Times-Picayune.*

"Do you mean to say the Governor of Louisiana can't even use the telephone, telegraph, or the United States mails because of the Klan?" Hoover exclaimed.

"That's just what the Governor told me personally when he sent for me to come to Louisiana," Wooton said. He gave Hoover a letter written by Governor John M. Parker of Louisiana. "I brought you this letter because Governor Parker can't trust the mails. His mail is watched by the Klan and his telephone is tapped by klansmen. He needs help."

It sounded fantastic, but it was true. The Governor was asking federal help to break a reign of terror by the Klan in northern Louisiana where its members were believed to have kidnaped, tortured, and murdered two victims. Law enforcement had broken down because police officers themselves were klansmen and people were afraid.

Finally, it was decided that Governor Parker should appeal for help directly to President Harding. This the Governor did on October 2, 1922, saying in part:

Due to the activities of an organized

**Post card printed shortly after rejuvenation of the Ku Klux Klan by Col. Simmons.**

> body reputed to be the Ku Klux Klan . . . not only have the laws been violated, but men taken out, beaten and whipped. Two men have been brutally murdered without trial or charges . . . my information tonight is that six more citizens have been ordered to leave their homes (in Morehouse Parish) under penalty of death. These conditions are beyond the control of the Governor of this State . . . a number of law officers and others charged with the enforcement of law in this State are publicly recognized as members of this Ku Klux Klan.

Parker asked for help under Section 4, Article 4, of the Constitution of the United States which guarantees all states federal protection against domestic violence, if an appeal for help is made either by a state legislature or a governor.

Agents were sent to Louisiana. To protect themselves, they had to work in secrecy but they found the Governor's story to be true. The Klan ruled with terror. Among the members were police officers, businessmen and well-known community officials. Women and men often were hauled from their homes in the night by hooded men, flogged, and even thrown into jail simply because the Klan ordered it. The klansmen themselves decided what was right and what was wrong, what was legal and what was not legal.

The agents gathered evidence that in August, 1922, klansmen—among them a doctor and a deputy sheriff—had kidnaped two men, tortured them to death

Klansmen picketing the *Atlanta Constitution*, Georgia daily newspaper opposed to the Klan. (From *Knights of the Ku Klux Klan* by Col. Winfield Jones, Copyright 1941.)

Burning a Fiery Cross. (From *Knights of the Ku Klux Klan* by Col. Winfield Jones, Copyright 1941.)

in the light of a blazing cross, and then thrown their headless bodies into the waters of Lake La Fourche. The bodies were found after a dynamite explosion had dislodged them from the lake bottom four months later.

Murder charges were filed but the grand jury returned no indictments because, according to the *Times-Picayune,* most of the jurors were klansmen.

Slowly, public anger built up against the Klan—stirred by newspaper crusades, prosecutions, and exposés such as the Louisiana case.

All through these years, the Bureau of Investigation itself was the center of bitter disputes. There were charges that government officials had used agents to spy on members of Congress who opposed them. One agent, Gaston B. Means, told a Congressional committee that he had broken into senators' offices, opened their mail, and looked through their desks in search of anything that might be used to embarrass them. There were even demands that the Bureau be broken up and its work placed under control of other departments of the government.

This was the low state to which a few men had brought the Bureau when President Harding died suddenly of an illness on August 2, 1923. Vice President Calvin Coolidge became President.

Coolidge, a sternly honest New Englander, was convinced there had to be a cleanup in the Department of Justice, which was being called the "Department of Injustice." He forced Attorney General Harry Daugherty to resign and in his place he named Harlan Fiske Stone, a former dean of the Columbia University School of Law.

One of Stone's first acts as Attorney General was to accept the resignation of William J. Burns as Director of the Bureau of Investigation. At a Cabinet meeting, he mentioned to Secretary of Commerce Herbert Hoover that he was looking for "the right man" to take over the Bureau.

When Hoover returned to his office, he happened to mention Stone's remark to his secretary, Larry Richey.

"Why should they look around?" Richey said. "They have the man they need right over there now—a young, well-educated lawyer named Hoover."

"You think he can do the job?" Herbert Hoover asked.

"I know he can," Richey said. "He's a good friend of mine."

Herbert Hoover told Stone of the talk he had had with Richey and suggested that Stone might be wise to give young Hoover a chance. He had been in the Department of Justice for several years and knew its problems.

The day after Burns resigned, Stone summoned 29-year-old J. Edgar Hoover into his office.

"Sit down," Stone said, looking at Hoover with a scowl. The frown was a habit with the big man who was over six feet tall and weighed more than two hundred pounds.

"Young man," Stone said, "I want you to be Acting Director of the Bureau of Investigation."

Hoover was so surprised he could say nothing for a moment. At last he said, "I'll take the job, Mr. Stone, on certain conditions."

"What are they?"

"The Bureau must be divorced from politics and not be a catch-all for political hacks. Appointments must be based on merit. Second, promotions will be made on proved ability and the Bureau will be responsible only to the Attorney General."

Stone replied: "I wouldn't give it to you under any other conditions. That's all, good day."

This interview took place on May 10, 1924, and on that day the new FBI had its beginning. Known for years as the Bureau of Investigation, it was later to be re-named the Federal Bureau of Investigation.

Soon Hoover was deep into the task of weeding out the incompetents and those who had held onto their jobs through political influence. One of the first to go was Gaston B. Means. Hoover made it a rule that new agents should be college men with degrees in law or accounting—for how could the guilt or innocence of a man be proved in court unless the facts in a case were gathered by experts? He saw the collection of facts as the key to justice in the courts.

Six days after taking over, Hoover sent a note to Stone saying: "I have . . . instructed the heads of the respective Divisions of the Bureau that the activities of the Bureau are to be limited strictly to investigations of violations of the federal statutes under your direction . . .

"I have already commenced an examination of the personnel files of each of the employees of the Bureau and have already recommended a number of Special Agents whose services may be discontinued for the best interests of the service. I shall continue to submit these recommendations to you . . . as rapidly as I can examine the personnel files."

It wasn't easy, getting rid of the deadwood. Senators and representatives complained when a relative or a friend was fired. One senator called on Hoover and demanded to know why an agent was being transferred from one city to another when the senator needed the agent to work for him in his coming campaign.

"I'm very sorry," Hoover said, "but I think it will be best for the agent and best for the Bureau if he gets away from his political ties. This will give him a new chance."

"I'll take this up with the Attorney General," the senator snapped, stalking from the office.

Later Stone called Hoover to his office. "Hoover," he said, "what are the facts in this case?"

Hoover explained his reasons for transferring the agent.

Stone said, "I think you are not entirely on sound ground."

As Hoover looked at Stone in dismay, the Attorney General said with a smile: "I'm surprised you didn't fire the fellow at once."

With Stone's strong support, Hoover laid down a stern code of conduct for the agents. In letters and instructions to his men he hammered on one main point: "This Bureau is to operate solely upon the basis of efficiency. Influence, political or otherwise, will not be tolerated and any Agent or employee of this Bureau resorting to same will be disciplined."

Many agents in the field paid no attention at first to the new orders coming from Washington. They figured it was just another "reform" wave that would soon be forgotten and things would be as they always had been. If they waited long enough, the whole thing would fade away.

But this time it didn't fade away.

Harlan Fiske Stone.

Hoover sent inspectors into the field to check each office and to report on the agents' efficiency, character, and industry. The rules were enforced. Office routine was made the same in every office. An agent shifted from one office found the same methods and rules when he arrived at another.

After watching Hoover at work for a few months, Stone gave him the full title of Director. Hoover demanded that agents conduct themselves properly on and off the job. On one occasion he wrote: "This Bureau cannot afford to have a public scandal visited upon it in view of the all too numerous attacks made . . . during the past few years. I do not want this Bureau to be referred to in terms I have frequently heard used against other governmental agencies . . ."

And so the new FBI shook loose from the tainted years of the past. Hoover had taken the job intending to remain only a short time before starting into law practice himself. Instead, he stayed on to guide the FBI through one crisis after another.

The change in the Bureau was so great that Harlan Fiske Stone (who became Supreme Court Chief Justice) was moved to write Hoover:

> I often look back to the days when I first made your acquaintance in the Department of Justice, and it is always a comfort to me to see how completely you have confirmed my judgment when I decided to place you at the head of the Bureau of Investigation. The Government can now take pride in the Bureau instead of feeling obliged to apologize for it.

# 5. The Outlaws Come to Power

In the Roaring Twenties and early Thirties, it seemed that the gangsters were more powerful than the law itself —until an aroused public demanded and got an end to the worst of the hoodlum terror.

The underworld grew into an invisible empire with its own laws, its own judges and executioners. It had squads of gunmen who were better armed, better paid, and better equipped than even the city, state and federal police officers. With threats and bribery, the gangs corrupted politicians, lawyers, doctors, judges, and law enforcement officials. The top leaders had their winter homes in Florida and used resorts such as Hot Springs, Arkansas, for their playgrounds.

Alphonse "Scarface" Capone came out of the New York and Chicago gutters to become one of the richest and most feared men of his time. The Chicago gangs at the peak of their power raked in from $100,000,000 to $300,000,000 a year. The money came from bootleg whiskey, beer and alcohol, and from robberies, gambling, and narcotics. It poured in from rackets. Businessmen were forced to buy "protection" and many labor unions slipped into the hands of hoodlums.

By 1926, homicides in the United States reached the alarming rate of 12,000 a year. Wholesale murders became common as gangland gunmen fought over the control of the rackets. In one thirty-month period in 1924-1926, Chicago alone had ninety-two gang-type murders. Only one out of ten was ever solved.

Crime was costing the United States billions of dollars each year. Worse yet, the underworld was allied with political machines across the country and, in many cases, with the police.

The FBI's hands were tied unless a federal law for which the FBI was responsible was broken. Murder, kidnaping, and terror in the cities were not federal offenses. They were violations of state laws for which the police were responsible.

For years it seemed that Al Capone was above the law and no one could reach him. But in 1929 he made the mistake which gave the FBI an opening. He was called as a witness before a federal grand jury in Chicago. When the time came for him to testify, he did not appear. His excuse was that he had been so ill with pneumonia in Miami that his doctor had ordered him to bed for six weeks. He filed a doctor's sworn statement that he was too sick to travel.

FBI agents checked on Capone's claims and found a quite different story. They discovered that during the time Capone said he was ill, he had been seen at the race track. He had flown to the Bahamas for a brief visit. He had also taken a boat trip to the British West Indies. And he had been seen at several places around town, looking in the best of health.

With this evidence, a federal court judge cited Capone for contempt of court in refusing to appear as a witness before the grand jury in Chicago. On March 27, 1929, he was arrested in Florida and released on $5,000 bail.

Before coming to trial on the contempt charge, Capone was arrested in Pennsylvania for carrying a concealed weapon and was sent to jail for one year. When he was released, he was jailed for another six months on the contempt charge.

During this time, the Internal Revenue Service had been checking Capone's lavish spending against the income he had reported in his tax return. They found evidence he had made a false report. He was charged with income tax evasion and sent to prison for ten years—the beginning of the end of Capone's reign of terror.

In New York, the most dangerous of the gang lords was a fawn-eyed, soft-voiced man named Louis "Lepke" Buchalter. He left a trail of dead men behind him for over ten years before he meekly surrendered to J. Edgar Hoover one August night as the FBI chief sat in his car a few steps off Fifth Avenue.

Lepke may well have been the most vicious criminal this country ever saw —and the most efficient. His crime syndicate became known as Murder, Inc., because it dealt in murder by the dozens. Yet for years Lepke managed to hide his moves so skillfully and with such secrecy that few people in New York knew he was the boss of rackets which produced a multimillion dollar yearly income.

Only a few knew that it was Lepke who coldly issued the orders for the murders of seventy or eighty men because dead men tell no tales. Those

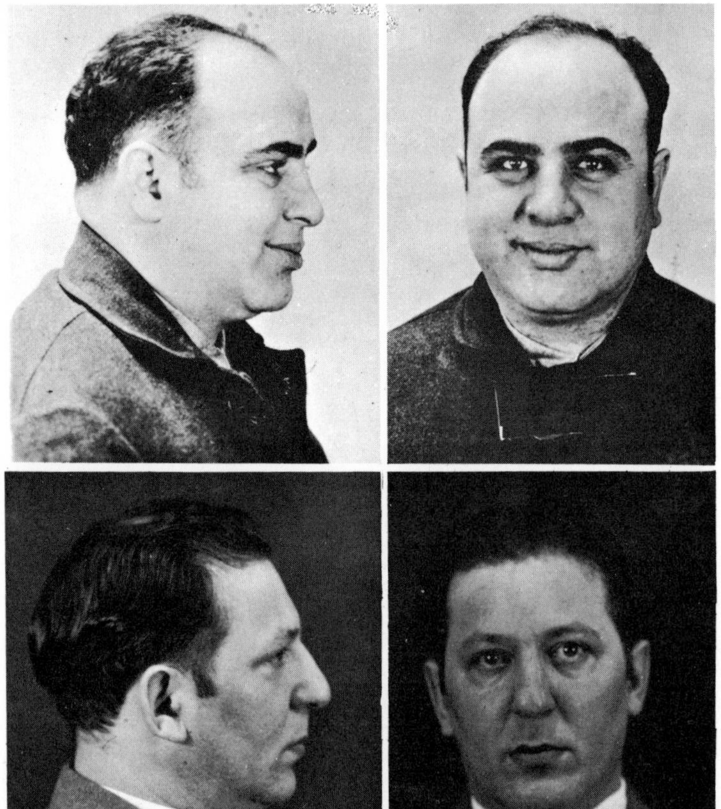

**Al Capone.**

**Louis "Lepke" Buchalter. His crime syndicate became known as Murder, Inc.**

gentle-looking eyes and the soft voice fooled a lot of people. But then Lepke was never seen around the favorite hangouts of the gangsters. When a day's work was done, he returned home for a quiet evening with his wife and son just as any other businessman might do.

Lepke was born on February 6, 1897, on the Lower East Side of New York City where his father ran a small hardware store. He was one of eleven children and his mother called him "Lepkeleh" (Little Louis), a name which his playmates soon shortened to Lepke.

His father died when he was thirteen and the family was broken up, although by this time Lepke already had decided to quit school. He worked for a time as a delivery boy and at other odd jobs around the tough neighborhood. When his mother left New York and moved to Colorado, Lepke refused to go along.

Police records show that in his late 'teens, Lepke had turned to picking pockets, stealing from lofts, and running errands for hoodlums of the East Side underworld. By the mid-Twenties he had risen in the ranks and become associated in a clothing company with a leading New York mobster known as "Little Augie."

Lepke was shrewd. He planned crimes so well that his admirers began to call him "the Judge" and "Judge Louis." It was a title of honor for the black-haired, neat little man. But he still was playing second fiddle to Little Augie.

Little Augie was soon removed from the scene. He was standing in a doorway one October day in 1927 talking to Jack "Legs" Diamond when a car swerved to the curb and a machine gun poured out a hail of bullets. Little Augie fell dead. Diamond was wounded but lived to write his own career in crime.

Police arrested Lepke, knowing so little of him he was booked as Louis Buckhouse. But they could prove nothing. No one could or would identify the men in the car from which the gun was fired. The police were forced to release him.

With Little Augie out of the way, Lepke began to run things as he thought they should be run. When labor leaders sent over a request for a squad of thugs to beat up the rebels who were making trouble for them, Lepke saw to it that his men did a good job.

Once the job was done, he did not accept his fee and call off his hoodlums as Little Augie had done. He installed his men in the union and saw to it that they were put into positions of power. They took charge of ballot boxes in elections. They voted to raise the members' dues—and those who protested were beaten. The increase in dues went into Lepke's pocket. The labor leaders were in no position to complain since they had started the whole thing.

Lepke used the same system when a manufacturer hired his men to break a strike or to prevent workers from joining a union. He gladly accepted the contract. When the job was finished he placed one of his lieutenants in the firm's business office to watch over the books. Lepke then took over the placing of contracts from which he got a kickback. The owners found themselves working for Lepke.

Lepke muscled his way into the fur, garment, baking, and trucking industries as well as dozens of other businesses while hiding his own role as the mastermind behind the schemes. Those who refused to coöperate were beaten, their merchandise was ruined by acid, or a bomb was tossed into their place of business. They lived with fear and violence until they agreed to Lepke's terms.

Lepke followed the simple rule that if there were no witnesses to a crime, there could be no indictment or trial. He sent witnesses out of the state under threat of death if they ever returned. When they disobeyed his orders, his killers hunted them down. His gunmen were paid a regular salary.

One of those who came back to New York was Max Rubin, a man who knew too much. Lepke had given Rubin money to go to Salt Lake City, then to the Catskills, and finally to New Orleans. Each time he was told to stay away, but Rubin always got homesick for New York and slipped back into the city.

The last time he returned, in 1936, Lepke sent one of his men to bring Rubin to him. The rain was pouring down that night as the hoodlum drove Rubin up Amsterdam Avenue. The car stopped near 150th Street.

"Get out," the driver said. "The boss wants to talk to you."

Rubin stepped from the car and saw the figure of a man standing beneath a dripping awning in front of a darkened store. It was Lepke.

"Why did you come back?" Lepke asked.

"I got homesick," Rubin said.

"How old are you?"

"I'm forty-eight," Rubin said.

Lepke said, "That's a ripe age, Max."

A few nights later a gunman held a pistol to Max Rubin's neck on Gunhill Road in the Bronx. He shot him and left him for dead. But Rubin lived. It was one of the worst mistakes Lepke ever made because Rubin's testimony one day would help send Lepke to the electric chair.

Lepke also helped organize a ring which smuggled an estimated $10,000,-000 worth of narcotics into the United States in 1936–1937. The key to this operation was two Customs inspectors who helped pass drug-filled trunks through Customs without inspection. They were paid $1,000 each time one of the trunks crossed the pier. For Lepke, it was a bargain.

At last, federal, state, and city officers began to close in on Lepke as more and more was learned of his operations. He was indicted for violation of the Anti-trust Act because of his control over the fur industry; and when the case was called for trial in 1937, he fled into hiding, ordering death for the witnesses who could be used against him. The underworld had never seen such a wave of murders as that which followed. Even Lepke's old pals were not certain who would be next—shot, stabbed in the back with an ice pick, or dumped at some lonely spot in the Catskills.

For almost two years Lepke hid while the manhunt went on. His name was among the top ones on the FBI's most-wanted list. New York's District Attorney Thomas E. Dewey put a $25,000 price on his head—dead or alive—in a drive to break the gangsters' hold in the city.

The underworld shielded Lepke for months. He hid in the Oriental Dance Hall in Coney Island for a time and then in a Brooklyn flat. When he tired of this place, he found refuge in an apartment on Foster Avenue in the

Flatbush district, posing as the paralyzed husband of a Mrs. Walker. But now and then he toured the city's streets, disguised only by a moustache and a pair of dark glasses. He continued to receive huge sums of money from his union victims and from businesses which he now owned.

Slowly the underworld turned against Lepke. He was too much of a millstone around the necks of too many people. The word got around that Lepke might be killed by someone in the underworld if he didn't give himself up.

Early in August, 1939, columnist Walter Winchell received a telephone call from a man who refused to give his name. The man told Winchell that Lepke wanted to surrender but was afraid because he had been told he would be shot "while trying to escape."

Winchell kept his friend, J. Edgar Hoover, advised of this call and others from the same man. As the days dragged on, Hoover's patience wore thin. He told Winchell to pass along the word that Lepke must surrender immediately. It was then that a plan was agreed on for Lepke to surrender to Hoover himself as a guarantee that he would receive safe conduct to jail.

On the night of August 24, the FBI Director sat in his car on 28th Street a short distance from Fifth Avenue. He had been there only a few minutes when Winchell walked up with a slender man who wore a moustache and dark glasses. They ducked into the car.

"Mr. Hoover, this is Lepke," Winchell said.

"Glad to meet you," Lepke said. "Let's go."

And so ended the hunt for Louis "Lepke" Buchalter, the "Judge" who had sentenced so many men to death. He was turned over to state authorities. Months later he was convicted in a New York court of ordering the murder of Joseph Rosen, a man whom Lepke had driven out of the garment business. One of the key witnesses against him was Max Rubin—the man his gunman had shot through the neck and failed to kill.

Lepke died in the electric chair at Sing Sing Prison on March 4, 1944.

Lepke, Capone, and others like them rose to places of power on a wave of unrest, confusion, and change which swept the country after World War I. One of the greatest opportunities for the gangsters was opened when the Eighteenth Amendment to the Constitution was ratified, making unlawful the manufacture and sale of alcoholic drinks.

The Treasury Department was given the job of enforcing Prohibition. A force of 4,000 "dry agents" was organized to stop the flow of whiskey and other spirits.

But though the country had voted dry, there were millions who simply ignored the law. The hoodlums quickly moved in to supply the demand for booze. Ships from England, France, and other countries—loaded with cargoes of whiskey and alcohol—anchored three miles offshore in international waters. They were beyond the legal reach of American law enforcement and their anchoring place became known as Rum Row on both the Atlantic and Pacific coasts.

The cargoes were unloaded from the ships into the fast, smaller boats of the rumrunners. Under cover of darkness, the bootleggers sneaked past the Coast Guard cutters patrolling the coasts—

sometimes engaging in machine gun battles. Liquor was smuggled across the Canadian border in huge quantities.

It was a dangerous business but it paid big profits. A case of whiskey that cost $15 could be sold for $70 to $80. A barrel of beer costing $3 brought $60. The trade ran into uncounted millions of dollars.

The gangsters now had money with which to bribe city officials, police, and federal Prohibition agents. A police officer or a federal agent earning $25 to $45 a week could make several hundred dollars in the same time merely by looking the other way when he knew the law was being broken.

There was one Prohibition official in New Jersey who complained bitterly that every agent in his office except three was taking bribes from the gangsters and that he couldn't "lead an army into battle" when most of his soldiers were in the pay of the enemy. The same kind of thing was happening in every state.

Early in 1925, officials in Cincinnati, Ohio, threw up their hands in despair and called on the Department of Justice for help in ridding the city of graft. The police themselves were allied with the crooks. Saloons were running wide open within two blocks of the Federal Building. The sale of narcotics was spreading.

Attorney General Stone called in Hoover to discuss what steps could be taken to restore decent law enforcement in Cincinnati. Hoover suggested the FBI send a special squad of agents to gather evidence, and Stone agreed.

The agents talked to hundreds of witnesses and persuaded scores of people to give them sworn statements. They got a confession from one narcotics peddler who admitted that in a thirty-month period he had taken in $455,056 and paid out $18,000 in protection money. The owner of four saloons taking in $3,500 a day admitted he had paid policemen some $200,000 over a span of three years. The agents got names, places, dates, and the amounts of money paid out.

In small towns on the edge of the city, the agents found many Justice of the Peace courts which were nothing more than racket centers. The "dry agents" were being paid a fee based on the number of arrests they made, plus a share of the fines.

The FBI had enough evidence for a crackdown in less than ninety days. A special federal grand jury met secretly and brought indictments against forty-eight Cincinnati police and twenty-three of the "dry agents." They were charged with conspiracies to violate the federal Prohibition and narcotics laws.

This time the accused men couldn't buy their way out by bribery. Some of them fled. FBI agents trailed them as far as Miami, Los Angeles, and Syracuse, New York. Out of the seventy-one who were indicted, seventy were tried and sixty-two convicted. The only one who wasn't brought to trial escaped into Canada.

Moving on the heels of this FBI exposé, the people of Cincinnati were able to force the old gang out of city hall and the police department.

Soon after this cleanup, Hoover was shocked by the news that a twenty-four-year-old thief named Martin James Durkin had shot and killed Special Agent Edwin C. Shanahan. He was the first FBI agent to be slain in line of duty.

**Special Agent Edwin C. Shanahan, the first FBI agent to be slain in line of duty.**

The FBI had been looking for Durkin for some time. Shanahan had spotted him sitting in a car and had moved toward him to make an arrest. Durkin grabbed a pistol from the car seat and sent a bullet smashing into Shanahan's chest.

Hoover called in an aide and said grimly, "We've got to get Durkin. If one man from the Bureau is killed, and the killer is permitted to get away, our agents will never be safe. We can't let him get away with it."

Hoover was determined to make the FBI one agency which would be feared by the underworld. Agents set out to track down the killer. They got on his trail when Durkin killed one policeman and wounded another in a gun battle in Chicago. They tracked him into California and lost all trace of him.

But then a Cadillac sedan was stolen in San Diego from the display room of a sales agency. The report of the theft sounded to the FBI as though Durkin might have done the job because he had used the same tricks before. They showed a picture of Durkin to a salesman at the agency.

"That's the man," the salesman said. "He was around several times looking at cars and asking prices."

From California, the agents followed Durkin into Arizona, New Mexico, and Texas. It was difficult work because the day of close coöperation between the FBI and local police had not yet arrived. Also, there was little teamwork between the police of one state and those in another.

The agents picked up the trail in one town only to lose it in another. The chase almost ended in Pecos, Texas, when the sheriff walked over to take a look at a new Cadillac parked on the main street. He saw a pistol lying between the man and woman sitting in the front seat.

"What are you doing with that pistol, young man?" the sheriff asked.

The man at the wheel of the car glibly explained that he was a deputy sheriff from California, passing through Pecos with his wife on his vacation. He said he had left his papers in his room at the hotel, but he would be glad to get them for the sheriff to prove he had a right to the pistol.

"I guess maybe you had better do that," the sheriff said.

Suddenly the driver started the engine and the Cadillac roared out of Pecos into the desert country.

The Pecos sheriff wrote a letter to the FBI office in El Paso describing the driver of the car. "I figured you just might have something on this bird," he said. The description he gave fitted that of Durkin.

FBI agents hurried to Pecos and followed the road Durkin had taken out of town. They found the Cadillac, badly wrecked, in a clump of mesquite. It was the car which had been stolen in San Diego.

A rancher living nearby told the agents that a man and woman had knocked at his door and told him a hard-luck story. They had asked to be driven to the nearest railway station. "I hauled them over to Girvin," the rancher said. "They were talking about going from Girvin to Alpine to catch a train."

Alpine was a town near the Mexican border but the agents were almost certain Durkin wouldn't head into Mexico or try to hide away in the desert. He liked the cities and night life too much. They questioned the ticket agent at the railroad station, giving him a description of Durkin and the woman.

"Come to think of it," the agent said, "a young fellow and a woman—he said she was his wife—got aboard No. 110 night before last. He bought tickets for San Antonio."

The agents questioned conductors, ticket agents, and porters. On the morning of January 20, 1926, they learned that Durkin and his girl were aboard the M. K. & T. "Texas Special" due to arrive in St. Louis at eleven o'clock that same morning. They phoned this information to the FBI office in St. Louis, giving the number of the car and the compartment occupied by the couple.

St. Louis agents got in touch with city detectives to ask their help. Odd as it might seem, the FBI agents could not arrest Durkin and charge him in federal court with the murder of Shanahan. Killing a federal officer was not then a federal offense. The killer could be prosecuted only in the courts of the state in which the crime had taken place.

Railroad officials had the Texas Special halted at a village outside the city.

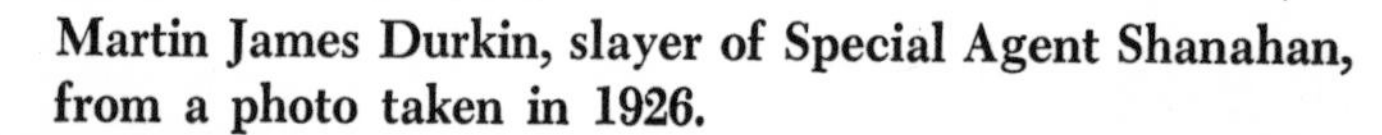
**Martin James Durkin, slayer of Special Agent Shanahan, from a photo taken in 1926.**

If there was to be any shooting, the agents didn't want it to take place in the crowded railroad station in St. Louis. Too many people would be in danger.

When the train came to a stop, the agents and detectives rushed aboard and burst into Durkin's compartment before he could reach for the pistols in his overcoat pocket. He was led from the train in handcuffs.

Durkin's arrest came a little more than three months after he had slain Shanahan. He confessed and was sentenced to a total of fifty years in prison —fifteen for a number of car thefts and thirty-five for murder. He was released in 1954 after serving twenty-eight years.

One of the strangest cases in which the FBI became involved in those years was that in which agents helped in capturing an army that was on its way to invade Mexico—a story that still would make a good theme for a musical comedy.

In 1924, Major General Enrique Estrada, who was Secretary of War in the government of Mexico's President Obregon, secretly plotted to overthrow the Obregon government. The revolt failed and Estrada fled with his friends into California. They settled down in Los Angeles to curse their bad luck and to make plans for the future.

The more they talked among themselves, the more they became convinced that they could overthrow the Mexican government. They figured that all they had to do was recruit a few men in Los Angeles, give them arms, put them into trucks, and lead them across the border. They would storm the Mexican garrison at Tecate, just south of the border. The news would spread. Recruits would flock to their banner, and the march on Mexico City would get underway, sweeping everything before it.

General Estrada did not bother to get in touch with any of the great arms makers to supply his army. He made a deal with a hardware store to buy guns and ammunition.

Also, he sent his recruiters into the Los Angeles Mexican colony to enlist men for the infantry. The promises of the recruiters went something like this: "Come with us. You will be paid generously. You will advance quickly in rank. And when the revolution succeeds, you will be given land and good jobs in Lower California."

The general and his friends spent about $62,400 for arms. For their money they got 400 Springfield rifles and 150,000 rounds of thirty-caliber ammunition; two Marlin machine guns; 5,000 rounds of machine gun ammunition; 300 pounds of dynamite, pipe fittings, and sheet iron with which to make their own aerial bombs; four Ryan monoplanes; two two-and-a-half-ton trucks with sheet iron sides; and five used trucks in which to carry men and supplies.

Now Estrada had an air force, an armored task force, 115 infantrymen, and a supply train. It was summer (1926) and the weather was ideal for making a surprise invasion. Few rumors of the plan had leaked to the Mexican government.

Unluckily for the general, the FBI received a tip that a revolutionary army was being trained and equipped on American soil to be used against a friendly neighbor. An investigation was ordered.

The spearhead of the army—an automobile and two trucks loaded with ammunition—moved out of Los Angeles on

Saturday afternoon, August 14. None was aware that the three automobiles trailing along at a distance carried FBI agents and Los Angeles police officers. The convoy halted for the night at Santa Ana.

Next day, the "troops" in Los Angeles were issued canteens of water, tobacco, and cigarettes. They piled into trucks and automobiles and drove south to join the spearhead unit at a point near the Mexican border. The infantry moved under the watchful eyes of FBI Special Agents James G. Findlay and A. A. Hopkins.

Before the invaders could cross the Mexican border, they were attacked from the rear by FBI agents, Border Patrolmen, police officers, and deputies from the San Diego County sheriff's office. Actually it wasn't an attack. The officers just moved in and put the generals and their troops under arrest without a shot being fired. Estrada was taken into custody by Agents Findlay and Hopkins.

The generals—there were four in addition to Estrada—were convicted of organizing a military expedition on American soil. They were sentenced to prison for terms of twelve to twenty-one months and fined from $1,000 to $10,000. As for the privates in this strange little army, most of them were sent home with a warning to behave themselves.

The capture of the army was an amusing episode—but there was nothing amusing in the crime problem as the Roaring Twenties came to an end. The gangsters still were riding high. Efforts to enforce the Prohibition laws were a disgrace.

President Herbert Hoover was so troubled that in 1929 he named a commission of well-known men to study crime conditions and to make a report. At the end of two years, the commission reported that blame for the crime situation had to be shared by the police, politicians, Congress, crooks, and the public.

The report touched off angry disputes and denials. But the most important thing it did was to underline the fact that crime was a problem which spilled across state lines. And the federal government had to do something about it.

# 6. Underworld Terror

A baby boy was kidnaped and murdered in New Jersey . . . Six law enforcement officers were shot down by gangsters' guns in Kansas City, Missouri . . . And a wealthy oil man was kidnaped from his home in Oklahoma.

These were the crimes in 1932–1933 which aroused such anger against the hoodlums that Congress passed special laws clearing the way for the FBI to plunge into gun-blazing, open war against the underworld.

The first shock came from news reports that a kidnaper had stolen the twenty-month-old, blue-eyed son of Mr. and Mrs. Charles A. Lindbergh.

Less than five years earlier, Lindbergh had flown across the Atlantic in his tiny plane, The Spirit of St. Louis. He had become the first man—flying alone—to span the ocean. Paris went wild when his plane touched down outside the city. Millions cheered him when he returned home to ride up Broadway in showers of ticker tape. He was hailed as a hero just as Astronaut John Glenn would be thirty-five years later.

Then he had married Anne Morrow and a son was born. They made their home in the Sourland mountains near the small town of Hopewell, New Jersey.

Early in the evening of March 1, 1932, the Lindbergh nurse had tucked blond-headed little Charles A. Lindbergh, Jr., into his bed, kissed him good-night, and left him snuggled beneath the covers. Silence settled over the house.

Soon after the lights went off in the second-floor nursery, a man moved from the shrubs outside carrying a crude, homemade ladder. He placed it against the house, climbed silently up the rungs to the unlocked window, and crept into the nursery.

He lifted the sleeping child from the crib. Little Charles made no outcry—at least none was heard. Then the kidnaper slipped back through the window, placing a note on the window sill. He eased himself and the child down the ladder and slipped away into the night.

When the nurse peeped into the room for a final look at the child around 10 P.M., she was stunned to see the empty crib. She spread the alarm. It was Lindbergh who found the note on the window sill which said:

> Dear Sir
>
> Have 50000$ ready 25000$ in 20$ bills 15000$ in 10$ bills and 10000$ in 5$ bills. After 2-4 days we will inform you were to deliver the mony. We warn you for making anyding public or for notify the police. The child is in gut care. Instruction for the letters are singnature.

At the bottom of the note were drawn two interlocking circles with three holes punched through the paper. This was the "singnature."

Lindbergh notified the New Jersey State Police. Day after day passed with no word from the kidnaper and no trace of the missing child. News reporters swarmed into Hopewell. People across the country eagerly grabbed each edition of their newspapers, hoping to read that the child had been found unharmed.

Dr. John F. Condon, a retired school principal, became the Lindberghs' agent in trying to make contact with the kidnaper. Using the name "Jafsie," Condon had a notice published in the Bronx, New York, *Home News* saying he was ready to act as the link between the kidnaper and the Lindberghs. Soon "Jafsie" was in touch with a man who called himself "John."

On the night of April 2—one month after the kidnaping—Condon slipped into St. Raymond's Cemetery in the Bronx carrying a package containing $50,000 in cash. From the shadows stepped the mystery man who called himself "John." Condon turned over the package of money after insisting on a receipt showing where the kidnap victim was. "John" told him the boy was safe and could be found on a boat named "Nellie" which was tied up at Martha's Vineyard, Massachusetts.

But there was no boat with the name "Nellie" at Martha's Vineyard. And there was no further word from the kidnaper.

The fate of the Lindbergh child re-

**Sketches of "John," who received the Lindbergh kidnap ransom money.**

mained a mystery until May 12, 1932. On that day a truck driver's helper noticed a small mound of dirt near a road only four and a half miles from the Lindbergh home. It was the shallow grave of Charles A. Lindbergh, Jr. The child had been killed by a crushing blow on his head.

Doctors who examined the body said he had been killed soon after being lifted from his nursery bed. He was dead when "John" told Condon in the cemetery that he would be found safe aboard the boat at Martha's Vineyard.

Discovery of the body sent a wave of sorrow and of outrage from coast to coast. One month later, Congress passed an act known as the Lindbergh Kidnap Law. This made the death penalty possible for anyone convicted of carrying a kidnaped person across a state line. Thus the door was opened for the FBI to enter kidnap cases.

The hunt for the mysterious "John" went on through the summer and fall of 1932. It continued through 1933 and on through the spring and summer of 1934, with every clue leading to a dead end. The New Jersey State Police were in charge of the case but they worked closely with the New York City police, the FBI, and other government agencies. Every clue was thoroughly investigated, and a special alert was posted for the ransom money. In fact, thousands of lists of the serial numbers on the ransom bills were published and distributed to banks, grocery stores, air terminals, department stores, and other establishments where the money might appear.

The first break came on September 15, 1934, in New York City. A motorist drove his car into a filling station in the Bronx and bought five gallons of gasoline. He handed the attendant a ten-dollar bill, received his change, and drove away.

But as the car moved away from the gas tanks, the attendant wrote on the bill the license number of the automobile—4U-13-41. He did this because the bill was a gold certificate—one of the kind which the Treasury had called in more than a year earlier when new paper money had been issued. If anyone asked any questions about the bill, the attendant wanted to make sure he could say where he got it.

The bill was deposited at the bank along with other money taken in by the filling station. On September 18, a teller at the Corn Exchange Bank and Trust Company spotted the old bill. He saw that it was the same type which the banks had been warned to look for in the Lindbergh kidnap case. A quick check of the serial numbers showed the bill was part of the ransom money.

The FBI was notified and the ransom bill was turned over to one of the City-State-FBI teams organized to concentrate on the kidnaping. A check with the State Motor Vehicle License Bureau showed that license number 4U-13-41 had been issued to Bruno Richard Hauptmann of 1279 East 222nd Street, in the Bronx, New York.

When Hauptmann was arrested, officers found in his pocket a twenty-dollar bill which also was a part of the ransom money. A search of his garage uncovered another $13,000 of the bills. Condon identified Hauptmann as the "John" to whom he had handed over the $50,000 in the cemetery.

Hauptmann denied the crime. But the evidence against him left no doubt with the jury that he was guilty. He was con-

**Bruno Richard Hauptmann.**

victed and on April 3, 1936, died in the electric chair for the murder of Charles A. Lindbergh, Jr.

The Lindbergh case led the FBI into strange byways. On one of these, FBI agents came across the tracks of Gaston B. Means—the same man who years before had been an agent in the old Bureau of Investigation and had admitted to searching the offices of senators.

Means was a crook and his reputation was well known. But for that very reason, Mrs. Evalyn Walsh McLean of Washington, D. C., thought that Means might be able to find the Lindbergh baby through his underworld contacts. She was a wealthy woman who was deeply touched by the Lindberghs' sorrow, and she wished to help.

Mrs. McLean telephoned Means and asked him to come to her home. The liar, rogue and ex-convict must have wondered why he was being invited to one of the most fashionable homes in Washington to talk with one of the city's richest women. But he hurried to keep the date.

Mrs. McLean came quickly to the point. She asked her visitor if he thought he could get in touch with the child's kidnaper and arrange for his safe return. Means said solemnly he thought it was a very strange thing that Mrs. McLean should ask him that question. It so happened, he said, that shortly before the kidnaping he was sitting in a New York saloon when he saw an old friend who had served time with him in the Atlanta prison. His friend had offered to let him in on a "big kidnaping job"—but he had refused.

When he read the news of the Lindbergh kidnaping, Means went on, he knew this was the job his friend had been talking about. Then he had checked around and learned that this fellow was a member of the gang which was holding the child.

"Do you think you could get in touch with them?" Mrs. McLean asked.

Means nodded. "I know I can," he said. And Mrs. McLean was convinced she had found the right man for the job. She told no one about the exciting game she was playing. There was time enough for that when the Lindbergh boy was returned to his mother and father.

Gaston B. Means

A few hours later Means made his first report to Mrs. McLean. He said he had been in touch with the kidnapers and they wanted $100,000 for the release of the child. He could do nothing without the money.

Still keeping her secret, Mrs. McLean got the money from her bank and turned it over to Means. He assured her he would not give the money to the kidnapers until they had delivered the child safely into her hands.

It was then that Means told Mrs. McLean of the secret code they must use in all notes and telephone calls. When he said anything about "The Book," he would be talking of the Lindbergh baby. Means would be "Number 27" and Mrs. McLean "Number 11." If he spoke of "The Fox" or "Number 19" he would be talking of the gang leader.

In some strange manner, Means was able to weave his stories into a believable tale for the woman who wanted so much to save the child. She received telephone calls at night from Means and from a man who called himself "The Fox."

Once Means brought "The Fox" to see her when she was at her country home in Aiken, South Carolina. The man wore gray suede gloves. When he touched the arm of a chair or the edge of a desk, he would carefully wipe the spot with a handkerchief as though his gloves would leave a telltale mark. He talked about ways to get the child to her without the police knowing it.

For weeks, Means continued the hoax. He brought Mrs. McLean stories of how the gang was trying to deliver the child but was being blocked by the police at every turn. He got her to give him another $4,000 for expenses and then insisted all their plans would be wrecked unless she paid the gang another $35,000. Success was always just around the corner.

Mrs. McLean was preparing to pawn her jewels to raise the money when her lawyer learned what had been going on. The FBI was asked to investigate.

Agents set out to find "The Fox." They checked on the long-distance calls which had been made to Mrs. McLean and to Means during the time the fraud was being carried out. Most of them were from pay stations. But on the night of March 23, there had been station-to-station calls a short time apart to Mrs. McLean and to the residence of Norman T. Whitaker. The Bureau's criminal records showed that Whitaker was an ex-convict and a disbarred attorney. He was arrested.

When Mrs. McLean saw Whitaker she identified him as "The Fox." Others in her household remembered him as the

**Photo of the jewels Mrs. Evalyn Walsh McLean, of Washington, D.C. planned to pawn to raise some of the ransom for the return of the kidnaped child of Col. Charles A. Lindbergh.**

man who came to the home in Aiken wearing gray suede gloves. Means and Whitaker were convicted of a conspiracy to commit larceny. Means was sentenced to fifteen years in prison and Whitaker to eighteen months.

By 1933, it became clear to more and more people in and out of government that the federal laws were not of much help in fighting interstate crime. The most effective law under which the FBI could act against organized racketeers was the Antitrust Act, but this was a law which had been passed to regulate big business—not to fight criminals. The criminals moved much as they pleased across state lines.

Banks were being robbed at the rate of almost two a day. Kidnapings had increased. Criminal gangs used fast cars with bullet-proof glass. They were well armed with machine guns and high-powered rifles.

But most of their crimes were not in violation of any federal law. And there were some odd twists to the law. For example, a bank employee who stole $500 or $1,000 from a federal bank was guilty of breaking a federal law. But a gang could rob the same bank of $500,000, shoot down its employees, and flee into another state without breaking a single federal law.

Also, the FBI's special agents had never been given full police powers by Congress. They could make arrests as any citizen can who witnesses a crime—but in most cases they were forced to ask the help of city and state police. Even then the agents found their plans were sometimes known to criminals within a matter of minutes. Too often the men they were after had a friend on the police force who tipped them off.

**Norman T. Whitaker, alias the "Fox."**

The FBI was still fighting crime with one hand tied behind its back when the gangsters sneered at the forces of law with the merciless killing that became known as the "Kansas City Massacre." It happened this way . . .

On June 16, 1933, FBI special agents came to the end of a three-year manhunt when they located Frank Nash—escaped convict and dangerous gunman—in Hot Springs, Arkansas. An arrest was not as simple as it might have been in another city because Hot Springs at that time was a favorite hangout for criminals.

Nash was among friends, and they were friends who would shoot to protect him if necessary. The agents felt they could not appeal to the Hot Springs police for fear Nash would be tipped off and the long chase would have to be started again.

With Police Chief Otto Reed of McAlester, Oklahoma, as a companion, two FBI agents waited in a car near a cigar store where Nash was chatting with a group of men. As the group disbanded, the agents walked up to Nash, grabbed him, and shoved him into their car. They sped out of Hot Springs, doubled back to escape any ambush by the gangsters, and drove to Fort Smith, Arkansas. There they boarded a train with their prisoner, heading for Kansas City and then Leavenworth Prison.

Hoodlums in Hot Springs passed along the word of Nash's capture to Vern Miller in Kansas City. Miller was a gunman and a pal of Nash's.

"Where are they taking Frank?" Miller asked the caller.

"They've got him on the train that gets into Kansas City at 7:15 in the morning," Miller was told.

That night Miller called together Charles "Pretty Boy" Floyd and Adam Richetti, two of the most dangerous men in the Middle West. They talked of ways to free Nash before he reached the gates of the prison. It was agreed that when the train arrived at Union Railway Station in Kansas City, the chances were Nash would be taken at once to a waiting automobile and then driven to Leavenworth.

"When they reach their car," Miller said, "that's when we'll jump them and take Frank."

That same night FBI agents and Kansas City police were making their plans, too. They decided that two FBI agents, Detective W. J. Grooms, and Detective Frank Hermanson should meet the train to aid the three men guarding Nash. The prisoner would be brought from the train to the car of FBI Special Agent Raymond Caffrey, who would be waiting in front of the station. Then Nash would be taken to prison.

The train arrived in Kansas City on schedule. The agents and detectives surrounded Nash and the group walked quickly among the early morning travelers toward the east end of the station. They crossed the street to where Caffrey's car was parked.

"Get into the front seat," Caffrey said to Nash.

Police Chief Reed and two FBI agents got into the rear seat where they could keep Nash covered. Caffrey walked around the car to slide under the wheel. Momentarily, the officers dropped their guard; and at this instant, three men suddenly appeared from behind nearby cars. Two of the men carried machine guns and the other held a pistol in each hand.

Kansas City, Missouri, Union Station Massacre.

One of the gunmen shouted, "Up! Up!" Then came a snarling command, "Let 'em have it." The blast of gunfire at close range ripped into the officers. Chief Reed, Detectives Grooms and Hermanson, and FBI Agent Caffrey fell dead. Two other FBI agents were wounded, one so badly that he would be forced to retire from the Bureau.

The killers leaped into their car and escaped, leaving Nash dead with one of their own bullets through his brain. But none of them was to live long. Two met violent deaths. The third was executed in the gas chamber of the Missouri State Penitentiary for his part in the crime.

The shock of the Kansas City Massacre had hardly worn off when gangsters boldly invaded the home of Charles F. Urschel of Oklahoma City and kidnaped the wealthy oil man along with his friend, Walter R. Jarrett.

During the evening of July 22, 1933, the Urschels and Jarretts were playing bridge on a screened porch at the Urschel home. Suddenly two gunmen, armed with a machine gun and a pistol, shoved open the screen door.

"Which one of you is Mr. Urschel?" a gunman demanded.

Neither Urschel nor Jarrett spoke. "Well," the gunman said, "we'll take both of you." He warned the two women not to touch the telephone. Then the men shoved their captives through the door. A car roared off into the night.

Mrs. Urschel ran at once to the telephone and called the special "kidnap number" which the FBI had urged people to use in just such cases—National 8-7117, Washington, D. C.

A switchboard operator at the Bureau relayed the call directly to the home of Director Hoover to whom Mrs. Urschel poured out her story.

Hoover called the FBI office in Oklahoma City and ordered agents to go at once to the Urschel home after alerting the Oklahoma City police. Other agents were sent from nearby cities. Their orders were to give every aid possible to the families but not to do anything that might endanger the lives of the missing men; if demands for ransom were received, the families should make their own decision whether to pay or not to pay.

Jarrett showed up at the Urschel home about two hours after the kidnaping, shaken but unhurt. He said the kidnapers stopped the car ten or twelve miles northeast of the city, robbed him of $50, and told him to get out. Then the car had headed south with Urschel.

The pattern was the same in this case as in other kidnapings. There was the agonizing wait by the family for some word. For four days they waited. Then a Western Union messenger delivered a package to a friend of the Urschels. The package contained one letter written in Urschel's own handwriting. Another letter, written on a typewriter, was addressed to E.E. Kirkpatrick of Oklahoma City, also one of Urschel's friends. Inside was a ransom note demanding $200,000 in cash.

The note said that if Mrs. Urschel was willing to pay the money for the safe return of her husband, she must place a want ad in the *Daily Oklahoman* reading:

> FOR SALE—160 Acres Land, good five room house, deep well. Also Cows, Tools, Tractor, Corn and Hay. $3750 for quick sale . . . Terms . . . Box H-807.

After the ad appeared in the paper, a letter came from Joplin, Missouri, with instructions on how the money was to be delivered. The following day, Kirkpatrick left Oklahoma City for Kansas City, Missouri. The handbag he carried was filled with packages of twenty-dollar bills. The FBI agents made no effort to follow Kirkpatrick, but they had made a record of the serial numbers of the bills.

On July 30—eight days after Urschel's kidnaping—Kirkpatrick registered as "Mr. Kincaid" at the Muehlebach Hotel in Kansas City. Late in the afternoon a man telephoned him and told him what he must do.

Kirkpatrick left the Muehlebach with the money and took a taxi to the LaSalle Hotel. He paid the driver and then began walking west as instructed. He had not gone far when a man walked up beside him and said, "Mr. Kincaid, I'll take that bag."

Kirkpatrick insisted that before he turned over the money, he had to know when Urschel would be freed. The stranger said, "The title deeds to the farm will be delivered within twelve hours." He took the bag and walked away.

This time the kidnapers kept their word. Urschel returned home the next night, tired but unharmed. After resting for a time, he sat down with FBI agents and told them what had happened—a story in which he revealed an astonishing memory for small but important details.

This was Urschel's story: After Jarrett had been robbed and put out of the car, the kidnapers had taped cotton and gauze over his eyes. Then they had driven steadily all night. At dawn, the car had swung into a garage or a barn, he couldn't tell which. The three of them got into another car which was much bigger than the first one, probably a Cadillac or a Buick. He was forced to lie on the floor.

After another three hours or so of driving, the car stopped at a filling station. He heard a woman's voice ask, "What can I do for you?"

"Fill 'er up," one of the men said.

As the gasoline splashed into the gas tank, the man said, "How are crop conditions?"

"The crops around here are burned up," the woman said, "although we may make a little broom corn."

The automobile pulled away from the gas station and they drove for another five or six hours. Again the car was driven into a garage or barn. Mr. Urschel asked the time, and one of the men said, "It's half-past two."

They gave him a ham sandwich and a cup of coffee, the first food any of them had eaten as far as Urschel knew. After nightfall they led him on foot to a nearby house where he spent the night. Next morning the men put him into another car and they drove for fifteen minutes or so to a farmhouse. He knew it was out in the country because he heard chickens cackling, hogs grunting, and cattle bawling.

He heard the sound of water being drawn from a well. He was given a drink from a tin cup which had no handle. The water had a mineral taste. It was in this house they took off the blindfolds long enough for him to write the letter which the Western Union messenger had delivered. He was in a bedroom, poorly furnished, with covered windows.

After the letter was written, the kid-

Bedroom in house of Armon Shannon.

napers blindfolded him again and handcuffed him to a chain. While unable to see, he carefully noted the sounds around him. Twice a day, he heard the drone of an airplane overhead. By subtle questions to his captors, he learned that the planes passed this spot at about 9:45 each morning and at approximately 5:45 in the afternoon.

He kept track of the days and on July 30, a Sunday, he heard rain beating down on the roof and pouring from the eaves of the house. He listened as usual for the plane to pass overhead but on this morning he didn't hear it.

The next day his captors put him back into a car and drove him to a point outside Norman, Oklahoma, where they freed him.

The FBI agents made a careful study of Urschel's story and the clues it contained. The woman at the filling station had spoken of a long, dry spell. Then there had been the sudden downpour of rain on July 30—and Urschel had not heard the plane that morning.

The agents checked with the airlines which had flights within 600 miles of Oklahoma City. The American Airways reported that on Sunday, July 30, the pilot on the Fort Worth to Amarillo flight had swung his plane north from the usual route to fly around a rainstorm. This point was marked on a map and then checked with Weather Bureau charts in Dallas. The charts showed that the area marked on the map had suffered from a long drought which was broken by a heavy downpour on July 30.

They found, too, that the American Airways' morning plane which left from Fort Worth usually passed near Para-

**Home of Armon Shannon near Paradise, Texas, where Charles F. Urschel was held for ransom in 1933.**

dise, Texas, about 9:45 A.M. The plane leaving Amarillo in the afternoon passed over this same point around 5:45 P.M. There was no doubt left. The kidnapers had held Urschel captive somewhere near the town of Paradise.

Agents found the two houses where Mr. Urschel had been held. They were on ranch land of the R. G. Shannon family. The water from the well had a mineral taste. The tin cup had no handle. There was a chain to which a man could be handcuffed.

Mrs. Shannon's daughter by an earlier marriage, Kathryn, was the wife of the notorious "Machine Gun" Kelly. He had once boasted he could shoot walnuts off a fence at twenty-five yards with his machine gun—and never touch the fence.

R. G. Shannon and his 22-year-old son confessed that they helped guard Urschel. They named the kidnapers as "Machine Gun" Kelly and his pal, Al Bates.

On August 12, Bates was arrested in Denver, Colorado, and $660 of the ransom money was found in his possession. Kelly and his wife were tracked across the country to a house in Memphis, Tennessee, the city where Kelly had once bootlegged whiskey into the city's fashionable homes.

A squad of FBI agents and Memphis police raided the house in the early morning hours of September 26, 1933. As they burst in on Kelly, he pleaded: "Don't shoot, G-Men! Don't shoot, G-Men!" And for years the FBI agents were known throughout the country as G-Men, Kelly's own term for government-men.

If any case ever underscored the interstate nature of crime, it was the Urschel kidnaping. The victim was seized in his home in Oklahoma City, Oklahoma, and carried into Texas. The ransom demand was mailed from Joplin, Missouri. Part of the ransom money was spent in St. Paul, Minnesota, and some of it turned up in Oregon. A bundle of the money was found buried in a cotton patch in Texas. Bates was arrested in Colorado and Kelly in Tennessee.

By this time the outcry against crime and criminals had become a roar of outrage. One senator wanted a bill passed by Congress to permit the governor in each state to name his own force of FBI special agents. Another plan was for the President of the United States to put the country under martial law and then send the United States Army into action against the hoodlums. Another would have placed all policemen under the control of the federal government.

Hoover fought against these moves which would have turned the police into a huge federal force directed from Washington. He argued that local police had the responsibility to enforce the laws of the states and it should never be taken from them. He favored new laws to give some muscle to federal law enforcement.

In May and June, 1934, Congress acted quickly. Nine major bills were passed giving the federal government more power in dealing with interstate crime. President Franklin D. Roosevelt signed them into law.

The passing of these laws was a turning point in the fight against crime. FBI agents now had full authority to carry firearms in line of duty and to make arrests without calling on local police for help. Now it was a federal crime to attack or to kill a federal agent, or to rob a federal bank. It was unlawful in some cases to flee from one state to another to escape trial or to avoid being a witness. It was against the law to carry stolen property worth $5,000 or more across a state line. Using interstate communications such as the telephone or telegraph for extortion was a crime. The kidnaping law was tightened up.

Now the FBI was ready for battle.

*Wide World*

**George "Machine Gun" Kelly and his wife, Kathryn, discuss tactics at their trial for the kidnaping of Charles Urschel.**

# 7. The FBI Fights Back

John Herbert Dillinger wrote his sister a letter in 1934 in which he said, "I am having a lot of fun."

The "fun" he was having was a crime rampage through the Midwest in which he and his gang left behind ten murdered men, seven wounded, a half-dozen banks robbed of tens of thousands of dollars, three police stations robbed of guns, and three jails from which they freed their friends.

They swooped into small towns like Old West outlaws, plundered banks, and shot their way out again. They did it without breaking a single federal law until Dillinger drove a stolen car from Indiana into Illinois—a mistake that would cost him his life.

Early in 1934, Dillinger was one of the most-wanted men in the United States. Among other crimes, he was wanted by police for the murder of an East Chicago policeman who had been shot down in Indiana. The Indiana police sent notices throughout the country asking other police to be on the watch for him.

The "wanted notices" on the Dillinger gang brought quick results. Late in January, Dillinger and three of his confederates were arrested in Tucson, Arizona. A fireman had identified two of the gang from their photographs and tipped off the police. At the time of their arrests, the four had more than $25,000, part of which had been stolen from an East Chicago bank. The gang also had five bullet-proof vests, three Thompson submachine guns, two Winchester rifles, and several pistols.

Dillinger was returned under heavy guard to Crown Point, Indiana. He was locked in the County Jail which, local officers boasted, was "escape proof." He was to be held there until time for his trial on a charge of murder.

On March 3, 1934, a jail guard opened the cellblock so that a morning clean-up crew could enter and found himself staring into the black muzzle of a forty-five caliber pistol. At least it looked to him like a pistol.

Using the guard as a shield, Dillinger captured five other jailers. After locking them up, he crept toward the warden's office and added another guard and a trusty to his growing list of prisoners. In the warden's office, he grabbed up two machine guns. In a matter of minutes, Dillinger had locked the guards and several unarmed jail trusties behind bars. He slipped out of the jail and headed for Chicago—driving a car stolen from the sheriff.

The guards swore that Dillinger had a real pistol in his hand when he escaped from his cell, a gun that must have been slipped to him from the outside. But Dillinger hooted that he had whittled a make-believe gun from a piece of wood with a razor blade—and this was the only weapon he had until he got his hands on the machine guns.

He wrote his sister:

> . . . (the reports) I had a real forty five Thats just a lot of hooey to cover up because they don't like to admit that I locked eight Deputys and a dozen trustys up with my wooden gun before I got my hands on the two machine guns. I showed everyone the wooden gun after I got a hold of the

Dillinger proudly exhibits the wooden gun he said was used in his escape from Crown Point.

Wide World

machine guns and you should have seen thire faces. Ha! Ha! Ha! Pulling that off was worth ten years of my life. Ha! Ha!

Perhaps it cost him a good deal more than ten years of his life when he drove the stolen car from Indiana into Illinois. In doing so, he broke the federal law known as the Dyer Act which forbids driving a stolen motor vehicle across a state line . . . and the FBI went after him.

Twice the agents thought they had Dillinger trapped. Each time he got away. Once Dillinger and his gang holed up at a summer place called Little Bohemia Lodge about fifty miles north of Rhinelander, Wisconsin. As agents crept toward the lodge at night, barking dogs gave the gang warning. They escaped from the lodge.

The officers raced through the dark woods pursuing the gang. Some of them ran into an ambush by Lester Gillis, known as "Baby Face" Nelson. Special Agent W. Carter Baum was killed. Another agent and a police officer were wounded.

In the two months following the battle at Little Bohemia, Congress passed the Crime Bills broadening the FBI's police powers. Hoover called Special Agent Samuel P. Cowley to his office and told him to take charge of the hunt for Dillinger. Cowley was a big man, thirty-four years old, and a former lawyer who once had served as a missionary in the Mormon Church.

"Stay on Dillinger," Hoover said. "Go anywhere the trail takes you. Take everyone who ever was remotely connected with the gang. Take him alive if you can but protect yourself."

Leland M. Benfer, *Milwaukee Sentinel*

**After the Battle of Little Bohemia. Sitting in the truck is one of the dogs which barked as FBI agents converged on the Dillinger gang.**

The trail led Cowley into Chicago where Dillinger was reported in hiding. There were rumors that a doctor had performed plastic surgery on his face to change his features. He was said to be in hiding until the scars were healed.

The FBI worked closely with two East Chicago policemen in trying to locate Dillinger. They were Captain Timothy O'Neill and Sergeant Martin Zarkovich, who had made many contacts with the underworld through the years.

On the evening of July 21, O'Neill and Zarkovich came to the FBI with a dark-haired, middle-aged woman named Ana Cumpanas. She was in trouble with the law and wanted to make a deal. If she received a reward and was not forced by the government to return to her native Rumania—as it appeared she might be—then she would lead the FBI to Dillinger.

Ana was promised a reward. Agents said they would do what they could for her on the deportation case, but they could make no promises because it was a matter in the hands of the Labor Department at that time.

Ana disclosed that Dillinger had promised to take her and a friend, Polly Hamilton, to a movie the next evening. She thought they were going to the Marbro Theater, but she wasn't sure. She would let them know the next day.

The question came up of how other agents and police officers, not in the

**Anna Cumpanas, the "Woman in Red," whose phone call to the FBI set the trap for Dillinger.**

room, would be able to identify her. The woman said she would be wearing a bright red dress.

The trap was planned. Early the next evening, Ana Cumpanas called to say that Dillinger would show up at either the Marbro Theater or the Biograph Theater. Plans had to be made quickly to have squads of men at both places.

In a final meeting, the agents were told:

> Gentlemen, you all know the character of John Dillinger. If . . . we locate him and he makes his escape it will be a disgrace to our Bureau. It may be that Dillinger will be at the picture show with his women companions unarmed—yet, he may appear there armed and with other members of his gang. There . . . will be an undetermined element of danger in taking Dillinger. It is hoped that he can be taken alive, if possible, and without injury to any agent . . . yet, gentlemen, this is the opportunity that we have all been waiting for and he must be taken. Do not unnecessarily endanger your own lives. If Dillinger offers any resistance each man will be for himself. It will be up to each of you to do whatever you think necessary to protect yourselves in taking Dillinger.

Dillinger decided at the last minute to see "Manhattan Melodrama," in which Clark Gable was starring, at the Biograph. Despite the surgery on his face, the agents recognized him as he walked into the theater with the two women—one of them "the woman in red."

Cowley called Hoover in Washington where the Director was waiting to hear how things were going. It was decided that the safest thing to do would be to take Dillinger when he came out of the theater rather than risk a gun battle inside. And so the agents waited.

The show ended and the crowd began streaming from the theater. Dillinger came out with the two women and as he walked from the entrance, Special Agent Melvin Purvis, who then had charge of the Chicago FBI office, lit a cigar. This was the signal for the trap to close.

Dillinger must have sensed at that moment that something was wrong. He looked quickly over his shoulder and saw an agent moving toward him. He ran toward an alley, clawing a pistol from his pants pocket. Three agents fired five shots and Dillinger fell on his face, dying. His "fun" was over.

*U.P.I.*

**On the sweltering night of July 22, 1934, Dillinger left the Biograph Theater, and turned to his left. He was killed by FBI agents as he ran for the alley.**

Hoover promoted Cowley to the rank of inspector for his work on the Dillinger case. And then the big man set out to run down the other members of the gang.

Four months after the Dillinger killing, he was driving along a highway near Barrington, Illinois, with Special Agent Herman E. Hollis. They passed a car and in that instant they saw that the driver was "Baby Face" Nelson whom the nation's newspapers were calling "Public Enemy No. 1." Nelson's wife Helen and a hoodlum named John Paul Chase were with him.

The agents wheeled their car around and gave chase. The gangsters pulled their car to the roadside and leaped out. Cowley and Hollis scrambled from their automobile and the gunfight started. Cowley and Hollis were killed.

Nelson, badly wounded, was dragged back into his car by his wife and Chase. The life slowly oozed from "Baby Face" Nelson as he lay bleeding in the car. When he died a few hours later, Chase and Mrs. Nelson pulled his body from the bandit car and left him lying in a ditch beside the road.

And then a curious thing happened. Nelson, who had slain three FBI agents, and Dillinger, whose gang had killed ten men, were treated by some people as heroes—and the FBI agents became the "bad" guys.

An editor in Virginia wrote of Dillinger's death: "Any brave man would have walked down the aisle and arrested Dillinger . . . Why were there so many cowards afraid of this one man? The answer is that the federal agents are mostly cowards."

A young girl wrote a letter to a Chicago newspaper saying, "I certainly feel sorry for his (Dillinger's) old father, and if I were a man and a member of Dil-

**"Baby Face" Nelson, a member of the Dillinger gang.**

linger's gang I'd certainly avenge his death."

A reporter in Chicago talked to "Baby Face" Nelson's widow and then wrote a sob story which said in part: " 'Baby Face' Nelson died in the arms of his wife with a smile on his lips, but with tears in his eyes for his two young children.

"Those were the highlights of a thrilling story told by Nelson's pretty widow, in which she gave a heartbroken account of his death at the hands of federal agents."

Only a bare mention was made in the story that Nelson had killed three FBI agents on his crime spree. Nothing was said of the fact that he and his wife seldom saw their own children who knew their mother only as "Aunt Helen."

Hoover was angered by such attacks even though the huge majority of people were on the side of the FBI. He called the criminals "vermin," "public rats," "vultures," and "scum." He made speeches attacking the lawyers, police, and politicians who allied themselves with the underworld. And he spoke out against easy paroles for those convicted of serious crimes.

Among those whom Hoover openly called a "rat" was Alvin Karpis, a killer who was known throughout the underworld as "Old Creepy."

For a long time Karpis was a member of the Barker-Karpis gang which was led by a woman, "Ma" Barker. She raised her four sons in Missouri and Oklahoma to be criminals, taught them how to use guns, and planned their crimes. She and one of her sons, Fred, were killed in a gun battle with FBI agents in Florida in 1935. She died with a machine gun in her hands.

Hoover's sneering remarks about Karpis being a "rat" enraged the hoodlum to the point where he sent word to Hoover that he intended to kill him at the first chance.

Quietly, the word passed among FBI agents that Karpis was "the Boss's man." Karpis was wanted for murder by state authorities and by the FBI for the kid-

**Three of the principal members of the Barker-Karpis mob.**

**"Doc" Barker** **Ma Barker** **Alvin Karpis**

**Arsenal of Kate and Fred Barker taken from their cottage in Florida after they were killed in 1935.**

naping of William Hamm, Jr., of St. Paul, who had been forced to pay $100,-000 for his release.

Agents trailed Karpis from Hot Springs, Arkansas, to Corpus Christi, Texas, and then to New Orleans. They sent word to Hoover that the gangster was living in an apartment house on Canal Street. Hoover immediately flew into New Orleans with a squad of agents. The FBI gave New Orleans police no notice. They took no chances that Karpis would be warned.

Hoover and his men were driving up to the apartment house when Karpis walked out of the building with one of his friends. For a few seconds a man riding a white horse along the street blocked the FBI cars.

Karpis stepped into his automobile. Hoover leaped from his car and ran to the left side of the gangster's car. He grabbed him before he could make a move for a rifle in the back of the automobile.

"Put the handcuffs on him," Hoover ordered. The agents who had gathered around the car looked at each other sheepishly. No one had remembered to bring handcuffs. An agent took off his necktie and tied Karpis's hands behind his back.

Karpis was put aboard a special plane to be flown to St. Paul, where he would stand trial for the Hamm kidnaping. The plane barely had taken off when Karpis's face turned a sickly white.

"What's the matter?" Hoover asked. "Are you airsick?"

Karpis blurted. "Go ahead and do it! Get it over with!"

"What are you talking about?" the Director said.

"I know what you're going to do," Karpis whimpered. "You guys are going to throw me out of this plane and then say it was an accident."

"Don't be a fool," Hoover said. "We don't do things like that. You're going to St. Paul to stand trial. Nobody's going to hurt you while you're with us."

Karpis was given a life sentence for the Hamm kidnaping.

These were hard, rough, and dangerous years for the FBI. But they also were the years when the FBI grew strong enough to fight the underworld on equal terms for the first time.

# 8. War and a New Enemy

The enemy's torpedo planes led the way, flying low over the dark blue waters of the Pacific. Behind them came the level bombers and then a swarm of dive bombers. The Rising Sun emblem of Japan was painted on the wings of each plane but there was no one on the waters below to see them in the gray light of dawn.

It was December 7, 1941. The planes were roaring in for the surprise attack on the great American naval base at Pearl Harbor in the Hawaiian Islands where the ships of the Pacific fleet rested at anchor.

The naval base and the nearby Army camps were slow in stirring to life this morning. It was Sunday and a day for the rules to be relaxed. Sailors and soldiers had been given their usual Saturday night passes to visit Honolulu, and many officers had gone to parties. No one knew that an enemy had been slipping across the sea for twelve days to strike the fleet a crippling blow.

The Japanese sea raiders had begun moving out of Hitokappu Bay in the Kurile Islands on November 25, 1941. The column of ships steamed toward Hawaii even while American and Japanese diplomats met in Washington, D. C., to talk of ways to avoid war.

There were six aircraft carriers, two of Japan's largest battleships, two heavy cruisers, supply ships, and a pack of destroyers to guard the column. The ships' radios were silent.

For six days the raiders churned through the sea without receiving orders. But on the seventh day a radio message came from Tokyo saying: "Niita Kayama Nobore!" (Climb Mount Niitaka —Proceed With Attack!) Now the ships ran at night without lights. Their orders were to turn back if they were seen by American ships or planes. If not—push on to the attack.

Commander Ono sat hour after hour in the radio room of the flagship listening to programs being broadcast from stations KGU and KGMB in Honolulu, only a few miles from Pearl Harbor. He heard nothing to cause him to believe the Americans suspected an attack from the sea.

Radiomen tuned in on the American pilots talking to each other as they flew scouting missions from the island of Oahu where Pearl Harbor was located. They made charts of the direction in which the planes flew and they noticed the planes always flew to the southwest. None flew to the north—the area into which the raiders were headed.

The ships steamed into position two hundred miles north of Oahu under cover of darkness. At dawn the torpedo planes and then the bombers took off from the decks of the carriers with their cargoes of explosives.

They came in low and swept across the island. Now the Japanese pilots could see their targets. The fleet was huddled at anchor in the harbor like so many huge ducks. Nearby were the airfields where Army, Navy, and Marine planes were lined up in neat rows beside the runways.

The first torpedoes and bombs began to fall at 7:55 A.M. At that instant—although none below could quite believe it for several roaring seconds—the

United States was at war with Japan. The raiders blasted at ships, planes, and airfields for 110 minutes before they swept back to sea and returned to the carriers.

In those minutes 3,435 men were killed or wounded. Eight battleships, three light cruisers, three destroyers, and four other vessels were sunk or badly damaged. A total of 188 American planes were destroyed. The enemy's losses were twenty-nine planes and five midget submarines.

As the bombs came crashing down and explosions jarred the island, Special Agent in Charge Robert L. Shivers in Honolulu managed to get a telephone call through to FBI Headquarters in Washington, D. C. It was about 2:30 P.M. in the capital. The call was switched to Hoover who was in New York City.

"The Japanese are bombing Pearl Harbor," Shivers told Hoover. "There is no doubt about it—those planes are Japanese. It's war. You may be able to hear the explosions yourself." The sound of explosions came clearly over the telephone.

Hoover issued orders immediately for the FBI to put into effect the war plans which the Bureau had prepared for such a crisis as this. Only two days earlier, the Director had sent word to his agents to be ready to arrest a total of 770 Japanese if the peace talks should fail and be followed by war. The agents in the field offices knew where each of them could be found. But no move could be made until President Franklin D. Roosevelt gave the orders.

The agents waited impatiently. An agent in San Francisco called Assistant Director Louis Nichols and said, "The boys are getting jumpy. Shouldn't we start moving?"

"Not yet," Nichols said. "We've got to wait for the papers to be signed after the President issues a proclamation. Don't take anybody into custody but go ahead and keep a watch over those on the list. Don't let those people get away from you even if you have to sit on their doorstep."

Early Sunday evening, President Roosevelt ordered that enemy aliens be taken into custody. Hoover sent an urgent message over the FBI teletype network:

> Immediately take into custody all Japanese who have been classified in A, B, and C categories. . . . Take immediate action and advise Bureau frequently by teletype as to exact identity of persons arrested . . .

On December 11, Germany and Italy declared war on the United States. Three days previously, the FBI's roundup of enemy aliens had been widened to include Germans and Italians. In the first seventy-two hours of war, 3,846 persons were arrested without violence.

The FBI went on a twenty-four hour schedule. All leaves were canceled. The nation was asked to strengthen its vigil against espionage or sabotage.

The first hint of spy work in the Pearl Harbor attack came even as the smoke of destruction hung over the mangled fleet. A thin column of smoke began rising from the yard of the Japanese Consulate in Honolulu. Consul General Nagao Kita and Vice Consul Atojiro Okuda were burning papers taken from the Consulate files.

It was natural that Kita wished to de-

Homes of alien enemies were searched by FBI for prohibited materials held in violation of Presidential Proclamations. Here is an assortment of prohibited articles seized in alien enemy searches in New York.

stroy the papers. They were secret messages he had exchanged with Foreign Minister Togo in Tokyo—messages which gave a last-minute report on the ships which were anchored at Pearl Harbor.

As Kita and Okuda desperately flung papers onto the fire, Agent Shivers called the Honolulu police and asked them to send a guard to the Consulate. When the officer saw what was happening, he ran into the yard and grabbed a handful of papers from the Japanese. Among the papers was a code book.

These were handed over to Shivers who gave them to the Navy to decode. Other coded messages sent by Kita to Tokyo were found in the files of the cable company office.

When the uncoded messages were brought to Shivers, he took one look through them and exclaimed: "My God! If we'd had these earlier! Look at this!" The messages read:

#0245 (1) "PA" 3 December, 1941

FROM: *Kita*

TO: *Foreign Minister, Tokyo*

(Secret Military message No.) (By Chief of Consulate's Code).

TO: *Chief of Third Section, Naval General Staff*

FROM: *Fujii*

Re signals I wish to simplify communications as follows:

1. Code (following 3 section 8 line table)
   1. Battle force, including scouting force, are about to put to sea—
   2. Several aircraft carriers plan to put to sea.
   3. All battle force has sailed 1st-3rd dates inc.
   4. Several aircraft carriers have sailed (1st to 3rd)
   5. All aircraft carriers have sailed (1st to 3rd)
   6. All battle force have sailed, 4th-6th dates inc.
   7. Several aircraft carriers have sailed (4th to 6th)
   8. All aircraft carriers have sailed (4th to 6th)
2. Signal

   Light in Lanikai beach house at night —

   One light from 8 P.M. to 9 P.M. indicates "1." From 9 P.M. to 10 P.M. indicates "2." The below signals until midnight, in order to indicate 3 and 4. Two lights, according to the time, indicates 5, 6, 7, 8. When not in accordance with (lights) above 1 full automobile headlight and one half light indicates 1, 2, 3, 4. Two full lights indicate 5, 6, 7, 8.

   2. On the Lanikai coast during daytime from 8 A.M. until noon every hour 1 piece linen cloth (sheet) indicates 1, 2, 3, 4. Two pieces linen cloth indicate 5, 6, 7, 8.

   3. In Lanikai bay during daytime in front of harbor (offing) a star boat with one star on sail indicates 1, 2, 3, 4; a star and "III" indicates 5, 6, 7, 8.

   4. Light in dormer window of Kalama house from 7 P.M. to 1 A.M. every hour indicates 3, 4, 5, 6, 7, 8. . . .

December 3, 1941

FROM: *Foreign Minister*

TO: *Kita, Consul, Honolulu*

Strictly secret

Would like you to hold on your list of code words (also those used in connection with radio broadcast) right up until the last minute. When the break comes burn immediately and wire us to that effect. *Togo*

FROM: *Kita* December 5, 1941
TO: *Foreign Minister, Tokyo*

1. The three battleships mentioned in your X239 of Friday morning, the 5th entered port. They expect to depart port on the 8th.
2. On the same day the Lexington and 5 heavy cruisers departed.
3. The following warships were anchored in the afternoon of the 5th:

8 Battleships
3 Light cruisers
16 Destroyers

Coming in were 4 cruisers of the Honolulu type and 2 destroyers.

*Kita*

December 6, 1941
FROM: *Togo, Foreign Minister*
TO: *Consul, Honolulu*

Please inform us immediately of any rumors of the movements of warships after the 4th.

*Togo*

The message of December 3 could mean only one thing: Kita had worked out a code by which someone could signal to a Japanese submarine lying offshore, giving reports on the ships at Pearl Harbor.

A house was found at Kalama with a dormer window. Its owner, Bernard Julius Otto Kuehn, was a German citizen. He also had a house at Lanikai, and nearby the agents observed a boat with a star on its sail—one which could be used to signal a submarine during the daytime from Lanikai Bay.

The FBI had been interested in Kuehn for a couple of years. He was a former member of the Nazi party. Even though he had no business of his own, the FBI knew he had deposited more than $70,000 in a Honolulu bank from 1936 to 1939. Kuehn's story to friends was that he had inherited money from his family.

In trying to find out where Kuehn got his money, the FBI began to suspect he had received it from Japanese in Berlin. The Army had information that Consul General Kita had sent a message to Tokyo asking if he could trust a couple in Hawaii named "Friedell." This message had been sent soon after Kuehn's wife had returned from a trip to Tokyo.

Agents were unable to find anyone in Hawaii having the name "Friedell" but they knew Mrs. Kuehn's first name was "Friedel," spelled with one "l."

Kuehn was arrested. He confessed that he worked out the code for Kita so that the movements of the Pacific fleet could be signaled to Japanese submarines. But he insisted the code was never used as far as he knew.

He told agents:

> . . . It was also arranged (with Kita) that this same set of signals could be given by short wave radio and arrangements were made that if the Consulate desired to contact me they could do so by sending me a postcard signed "Jimmie," to my Box No. 1476 at Honolulu . . . On the same occasion that I transmitted this simplified system of signaling I had also advised the Consulate that there were seven battleships, six cruisers, two aircraft carriers, forty destroyers, and twenty-seven submarines, or some similar figure, in Hawaiian waters . . .

Kuehn admitted he received some $30,000 in 1940–1941 from persons in Tokyo. He claimed it was from property he owned in Berlin. He told a story of receiving one $14,000 payment from a Japanese he had never seen before. He said his wife had hidden the money.

"I don't know where she has it hidden," Kuehn said.

Agents had reason to believe that the "stranger" who handed Kuehn the $14,000 worked at the Japanese Consulate in Honolulu, and that he was an aide of Vice Consul Okuda.

By the time Kuehn was arrested, Hawaii was under martial law because of the fear of another Japanese attack. A military court sentenced Kuehn to be shot. But the sentence was later softened to imprisonment and after the war Kuehn left the United States on parole.

Kuehn was one of ninety-one persons convicted of spying against the United States from 1938 to 1945—and two-thirds of them were American citizens. Some became spies out of loyalty to Germany. Some were recruited by the Nazis by means of threats against their families. Others became enemy agents for the money they could make.

Adolph Hitler's Nazi agents tried to set up spy and sabotage rings in the United States as the Germans had done with such success in World War I. But the effort failed. One reason was because the FBI—long before the attack on Pearl Harbor—had begun secretly to look into the activities of people known to be Communists and Fascists.

This undercover work had its start on August 24, 1936, when Director Hoover answered a call from the White House asking him to come to the office of President Roosevelt.

It was 9:15 A.M. when Hoover was shown into a room in the west wing of the White House. The President looked up from his desk and smiled. "Sit down, Edgar," he said, lighting a cigarette.

"I called you over," Roosevelt said, "because I want you to do a job for me and it must be confidential."

The President then explained that he was troubled by reports he had received from people who were worried by the activities of Communist and Fascist groups. He thought he should know more of what these people were doing —and why. But the President wanted no one to know an investigation was being made.

Hoover said there was no agency in the government gathering information on subversive activities. It was not against the law to belong to the Communist Party or to be a Fascist. And Congress had never given the FBI authority to check on such matters.

Roosevelt said, "It seems to me there must be some way this could be done, Edgar. Have you any suggestions?"

"Yes, there is a way," Hoover said. "The FBI can make an investigation for the Department of State when requested to do so by the Secretary of State. We could make the investigation should the Secretary request it of the Attorney General."

The President said he didn't wish to make a formal, written request of the State Department. There was too much risk of a leak. To remove any doubt about the FBI's authority, he said he would write a note and put it in his safe, saying that he had asked Secretary of State Cordell Hull to make the request of the FBI.

"I want you to come back tomorrow and talk this over with Cordell and me," Roosevelt said.

Hoover returned to the White House the following day at 1:45 P.M. and was joined by Secretary Hull. Roosevelt explained to Hull what he wished to do

**Propaganda material and membership books of Nazi organizations seized in alien enemy searches in San Francisco.**

and then added: "Edgar says he can do this but the request must come from you to make it legal."

Hull turned to Hoover. He said: "Go ahead and investigate!" And the President threw back his head and laughed.

Hull's request for the investigation was passed on by Hoover to Attorney General Homer Cummings when Cummings returned to his office from a trip. "Go ahead with the investigation by all means," Cummings said.

Then it was that FBI agents—fresh from the gang wars—also took on the job of checking into the secret activities of the Communist and Fascist groups around the country. When war broke out in Europe in 1939, Roosevelt made the FBI responsible for foreign intelligence work in the Western Hemisphere, including the United States, Central America, the Caribbean, and South America. The Army and Navy were responsible for gathering intelligence in other parts of the world.

One of the strangest spy dramas began in 1940 when William Sebold, a German who had become an American citizen, was met aboard the S.S. *President Washington* by an FBI agent as the ship arrived in New York. Sebold was returning from Germany, where he had

**Guns and equipment seized in alien enemy searches in St. Louis area.**

gone for a visit with his relatives. One day during his stay there he was contacted by members of Hitler's Gestapo—the dreaded secret police of the Nazis. The Gestapo men threatened to make life miserable for his family unless he returned to the United States as a spy for Germany.

Sebold told the Gestapo he would do whatever had to be done. He was then sent to Klopstock Pension in Hamburg where the Germans ran a school for their espionage agents. He was taught how to use a short-wave radio and how to write and read messages with a secret code. He also was given messages to be passed on to other German agents.

The Nazis sent Sebold back to the United States, certain they had found a valuable agent. But Sebold hated the Nazis and he knew that nothing he did would give his family any guarantee of safety. He told the whole story to the FBI—and then agreed to play the role of a spy in an effort to trap other German agents.

The FBI arranged for Sebold to send a coded message to the Nazi radio station at Hamburg saying he had arrived safely.

Agents began at once to furnish an office for Sebold in midtown Manhattan. They placed a trick mirror in one wall. Anyone looking into the mirror from the office saw only an image of himself and a reflection of the room behind him. But agents in the next room could look through the mirror and take movies of everything going on in the office. They hid microphones so they could listen to every word spoken.

The agents hung a calendar on the wall behind Sebold's desk chair. A clock was placed on the desk near the chair

**Duquesne case—FBI agent taking movies through two-way mirror.**

in which any visitor would sit. Thus the camera behind the mirror could film the date, the time, and the face of every visitor while agents made a record of anything said.

FBI Laboratory engineers built a short-wave radio station at Centerport, Long Island. It was registered with the government as an amateur station just in case anyone became suspicious.

At 7:50 P.M. on May 20 the FBI was ready. Radio contact was made with the station in Hamburg. Agents began feeding a steady stream of information to the Germans in the weeks that followed. But all the messages had been approved

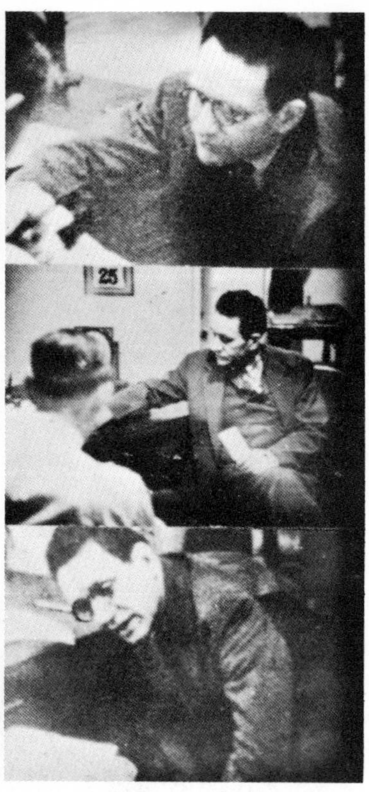

**Fritz Duquesne in office of William Sebold taken through two-way mirror.**

by Army and Navy Intelligence officers.

Sebold got in touch with other German agents. They called at his office to ask for instructions or to turn over to him messages to be sent to Germany. All the while FBI agents were recording each meeting from their posts behind the mirror.

One of those who called on Sebold was Fritz Duquesne. He had spied against the British during the Boer War and was strongly pro-German in World War I. Now he was the leader in a new spy ring which the Germans were trying to organize. His special interest was to give Germany everything he could find out about ships sailing to and from England, how many planes were going to the British, the rate of American military production, and the training of United States airmen.

The game continued until the FBI was certain that it knew the names and faces of everyone in the spy ring. Then the trap was sprung. Thirty-three persons, including Duquesne, were convicted of espionage or a related charge. As one agent remarked, "It was like shooting fish in a barrel."

When the crackdown came, the radio station on Long Island had sent and received more than 500 messages, with the Germans none the wiser that Sebold was working for the FBI.

The Germans tried many espionage tricks before and during World War II, but one of the cleverest of all was the use of tiny photographs which became known to the FBI as "micro-dots."

The first warning that the Germans were going to use this method of passing information from agent to agent came from a double-agent—a man who pretended to work for the Germans but who reported to the FBI. This man had been a student at the spy school at Klopstock Pension where he was shown an amazing invention to be used by Nazi spies. It was a process by which a full-page letter could be reduced to a size smaller than a pin-head. The trick was done with photography—but that's all the man knew.

With this warning, the FBI set out to learn the German secret. A few months later, a man arrived in New York from South America and met with two FBI agents in a hotel room. He turned over to them four telegraph blanks.

"Here they are," he said. The agents studied the blanks closely but they could find nothing unusual about them.

The blanks were sent to the FBI Laboratory in Washington. When a technician placed the paper under a fluorescent lamp, he saw several tiny black dots embedded in the paper. Carefully, he pried one of them loose. He placed it under a microscope which enlarged it two hundred times. The "dot" was a full-page message—as were other dots on the telegraph blanks.

The discovery of this secret helped the FBI break up spy rings in this country as well as in Mexico and South America.

Of all the double agents, none was more successful than a man known to this day only as ND98. He had an import-export business in Germany when he was recruited by the Nazis as an espionage agent. He was given the usual training in secret writing, radio, and codes. His orders were given to him on the easily-hidden micro-photographs.

In 1941, after his training ended, he was called to the office of a Nazi official in Hamburg who told him: "You will go to Uruguay and set up a radio transmitter. Here are the names of three persons who will send you information from America concerning war production and military installations. Contact us when you have the radio ready. Here are your papers and instructions."

ND98 went by ship to Montevideo. Secretly, he met a U. S. State Department official and offered—for a price—to work for the United States. His offer was accepted and things moved quickly after that.

A few days later he sent a message to his Nazi bosses:

> Impossible to establish radio station and obtain information desired. Am going to United States where I will be able to operate more freely. Will contact you.

When ND98 arrived in New York, he was met by FBI agents. Once again a secret radio station was set up on Long Island. ND98 made his first radio contact with the Hamburg station on February 20, 1942. He was told to get information as quickly as possible on aircraft, ship and arms production, troop movements, shipping, and any new weapons being developed in the United States.

Once again military men supplied information which they wished to be passed on to the Germans. ND98 sent it to the Hamburg station.

Things went so well that the FBI thought the time had come to use the station as a trap for other Nazi agents. ND98 sent a message saying: "Urgently need help. Can you have reliable agents report to me?"

It didn't work. The station in Hamburg replied: "You and your work too valuable to have you identified with anyone else."

Several months later the Hamburg station sent a grumbling message saying ND98's information was very good—but it was costing too much. He had been paid $34,000 (which the FBI had turned over to the government).

ND98 replied: "Sorry you regard information as too expensive. If not satisfactory, will be glad to withdraw as strain and danger are great." The German station hurriedly replied that $20,000 more was being sent to him at once and he must continue on the job.

In November of 1943, ND98 hinted in a message to Hamburg that United States forces in the Pacific were planning a big attack on the Northern Kurile Islands—a message dangerously near the truth. Actually, the attack on the Kuriles was to cover up the main blow which was to be aimed against the Marshall Islands.

The Germans did as the American military men hoped they would. They relayed ND98's warning to Japan—and there was reason to believe the Japanese were thrown off guard when the attack was made on the Marshalls in February, 1944.

ND98 sent a series of messages to the Germans in the spring of 1944, to confuse them over the Allies' plans for invading France. One message said the invasion had been delayed by a breakdown in the building of assault boats. Another said that infantry and armor were being moved to the Mediterranean "for a special operation" and that ND98 "will make every effort to ascertain further details."

Even after the invasion of France on June 6, ND98 kept his radio contact with the Hamburg station. It continued until Hamburg was captured by the British on May 2, 1945.

The government paid ND98 a total of $32,000 in salary, bonuses, and expenses. But it was a bargain because the Germans had sent over $55,000 to keep him in business and this was more than enough to pay for the operation.

# 9. Saboteurs Land from the Sea

One night in May, 1942—a little more than five months after the Japanese attack on Pearl Harbor—a German submarine slipped out of the U-boat base at Lorient, France, and set out for the east coast of the United States. Two nights later the submarine *Innsbruck* left its concrete pen at the big base and headed in the same direction.

The U-boats ran on the surface of the ocean at night when there was no danger of being seen. But when day came they ran submerged to hide themselves from any British or American warships or planes that might cross their path. At times only their periscopes showed.

Each submarine carried a four-man team of saboteurs. The teams' mission was to slip into the United States and then—with fire bombs and explosives—destroy aluminum plants, river locks, railroad bridges, and factories important to the American war effort.

This daring plan had its beginning in 1940. By this time Nazi leaders were grumbling that the Abwehr—the Nazi intelligence service—had no agents in the United States who could be depended on to carry out espionage and sabotage. The Germans in World War I had had great success in damaging or destroying American ships, ammunition dumps, and war plants. The Nazis saw no reason why the same thing could not be done again.

The Abwehr chiefs were in trouble because the agents they had trained so carefully were being arrested faster than they could be replaced.

By mid 1941, even Fritz Duquesne, one of their most able operators, had been caught by the FBI and was in jail.

Under pressure to do something, the Abwehr chiefs decided to train new men and to send them across the Atlantic in submarines. They could be landed on a lonely stretch of beach with their supplies. Then they would split up into pairs and go about their work.

The plan was taken to Admiral Doenitz. He wasn't happy at first with the idea of risking two of his badly-needed submarines on such a mission. But at last he agreed when the Abwehr promised that only the best agents would be chosen to do the work—and they would pass along information useful to the German Navy and to the U-boats in the Atlantic.

The Abwehr gave the task of recruiting the agents to fat, thick-necked Lieutenant Walter Kappe. Kappe had once lived in Chicago where the FBI knew him as a leader in pro-Nazi associations. He had left the United States in 1937 to return to Germany and enter the Intelligence service.

Kappe talked with dozens of men before he found the eight men he believed to be the best for the job. Each of them had once lived in the United States. They knew the country well and they spoke English with little if any trace of a German accent. They were men who would have no trouble passing themselves off as Americans.

The oldest of the group was George Dasch who was thirty-nine. He had once made all the moves toward becoming an American citizen except the final one of swearing allegiance to the United States. Before he could take the oath, war had started in Europe. He had decided to return to Germany and the cost of his passage was paid by the German government.

The eight men were sent to a Nazi sabotage school at Quentz Lake near Berlin. There they learned how to use explosives, fire bombs, detonators, and timing devices. They memorized false stories of their lives. Experts in forgery supplied them with false birth certificates, Social Security cards, drivers' licenses, and cards showing they had been deferred from serving in the American armed forces.

At last the men were taken to the submarine base at Lorient. Dasch headed the team of Ernest Burger, thirty-five; Heinrich Heinck, thirty-four, and Richard Quirin, thirty-four. Edward Kerling, thirty-two, had on his team Herman Neubauer, thirty-two; Werner Thiel, thirty-five; and Herbert Haupt, twenty-two.

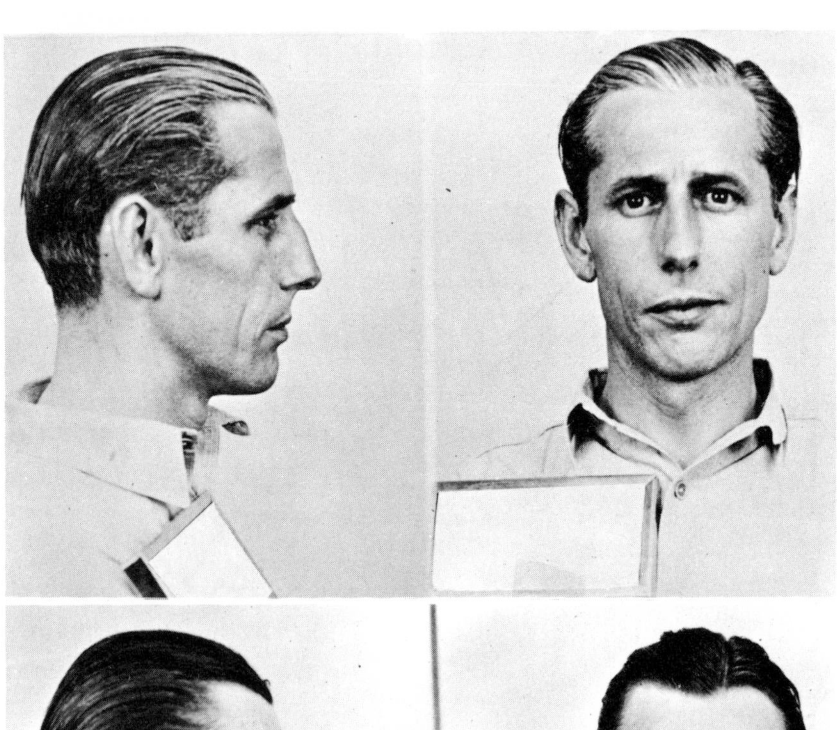

George John Dasch.

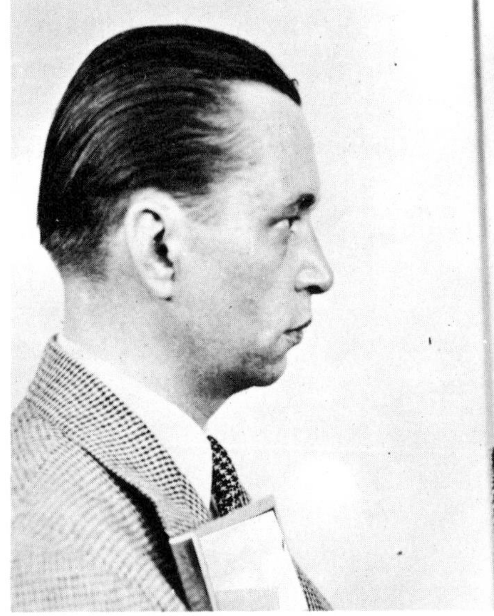

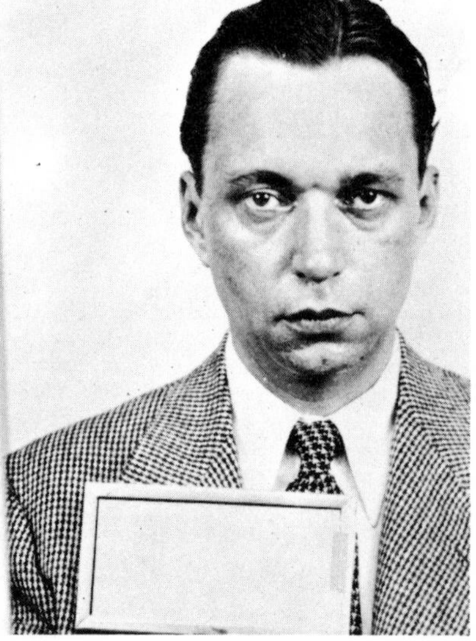

Ernest Peter Burger.

Kappe gave Dasch and Kerling each $50,000 to be used as a general fund, and each got $20,000 for expenses. Also each man received a money belt containing $4,000 and a wallet filled with $400 in small bills. In all, they carried $175,200 which was supposed to last them for two years. Most of the money was in fifty-dollar bills.

Each team carried aboard the submarines four water-proof boxes filled with powerful explosives, TNT bombs which looked like chunks of coal, fuses, chemicals, and other sabotage equipment.

Their main targets were to be the Aluminum Company of America plant at Alcoa, Tennessee; an aluminum plant at East St. Louis, Illinois; the Cryolite plant at Philadelphia; locks on the Ohio river; the Pennsylvania railroad station at Newark, New Jersey; and bridges and equipment on the major railroads in the East.

Sixteen days after leaving Lorient—near midnight on June 12—the U-boat *Innsbruck* came to the surface of the ocean not far from Amagansett, Long Island. The skipper had set a course for East Hampton but the lights on the shore were blotted out by a heavy fog and he was three miles off his target.

The commander decided to get the saboteurs ashore without delay. He moved the U-boat to a point about 440 yards from the beach and cut the engines. Seamen climbed through the hatchway and inflated a rubber boat.

Talking in whispers, Dasch led his men into the boat. They wore the work uniforms of German Marines. Two seamen rowed them ashore and they scrambled through the surf onto the beach. In the excitement, the seamen dropped their oars and the boat was swamped in shallow water.

Dasch and his men carried the equipment ashore. They stripped off their wet uniforms and began changing into civilian clothes while the seamen struggled to empty the water from their boat.

The saboteurs might have landed that night with no one the wiser except for the U-boat commander's small error in navigation. It happened that as the rubber boat carried the four saboteurs toward the beach, a young Coast Guardsman stepped out of the Amagansett Coast Guard Station to make his usual midnight beach patrol.

Seaman 2/c John Cullen walked through the fog alone and unarmed. It didn't seem necessary to carry a weapon to patrol this strip of beach where nothing ever happened. The beam of his flashlight cut a cone of light into the gray fog, but only for a few yards. There was silence except for the lapping of the water on the beach and the crunch of his shoes in the sand.

It was Dasch who saw the blob of light coming toward him and his companions through the mist. He walked quickly toward Cullen to stop him before he could see the seamen working to get their boat off the beach.

"What's going on here?" demanded Cullen. "Who are you?" He saw that two men were working with something at the edge of the water.

"There's nothing wrong," Dasch said. "We're fishermen. Our boat ran aground and we're going to wait here until daylight."

He explained they had become lost in the fog while heading from East Hampton for Montauk Point. He asked where they were. Cullen told him they were three miles from East Hampton.

Cullen said: "It will be four hours until sunup. You had better come with me to the station."

Dasch started up the beach with Cullen. For a moment he thought of slugging the young man and forcing him to go aboard the submarine as a prisoner. But then he decided to try bribery.

He stopped and said to Cullen: "Wait a minute. I'm not going with you."

"You'll have to go," the youth said stubbornly.

"Now, listen," Dasch said. "How old are you? Do you have a father and mother? I don't want to kill you. You don't know what this is all about. Why don't you forget it? Here is some money. Go out and have yourself a good time."

"I don't want the money," Cullen said.

From out of the fog a man ran up to Dasch and said something in German. Dasch snapped, "Shut up!" He slapped his hand over the man's mouth.

Dasch turned on Cullen and grabbed him by the arm. He shoved a wad of money into his hand and demanded: "Look in my eyes! Look in my eyes! Would you know me if you ever saw me again?"

"No," Cullen said. "I have never seen you before."

"You might see me in East Hampton."

"I never saw you," the youth said, backing away—not knowing how many men were around him in the fog. He turned and ran for the Coast Guard station to report what had happened.

When Dasch returned to his companions, the boat was gone. He said: "It's all right. I fixed everything."

The saboteurs carried their uniforms and supplies into the dunes. They buried them in the sand near a post which could be used as a marker when they returned for them later. Then they walked from the beach until they came to a paved road. They hid near the road waiting for daybreak.

When dawn came, the four Germans walked across the fields to the Long Island Rail Road tracks. They followed the tracks to the station at Amagansett. The station was locked but the ticket agent showed up after a few minutes.

"You're out early this morning," the agent said.

"Yes," Dasch said, "we've been fishing."

The saboteurs boarded the 6:57 train and rode into New York City. Dasch and Burger went to the Governor Clinton Hotel and Heinck and Quirin to the Hotel Martinique.

But while the four of them were leaving the beach, young Cullen was at the Coast Guard station telling his story to four Guardsmen on duty. He showed them the handful of money, $260. Quickly, the men armed themselves and went to the spot where Cullen had met Dasch. They found nothing, but they did hear the sound of engines coming from the ocean.

Cullen said later: "Three of us laid around on the top of the beach where I had seen him (Dasch). We stayed there for a while and then we heard these motors out in the water, but we couldn't see anything. We thought they were coming back . . . The motors cut off and we did not hear them. . . ."

The motors they heard were those of the *Innsbruck* which was stuck on a sandbar and held fast until it floated free with the incoming tide.

When daylight came, the Guardsmen searched the beach again. This time

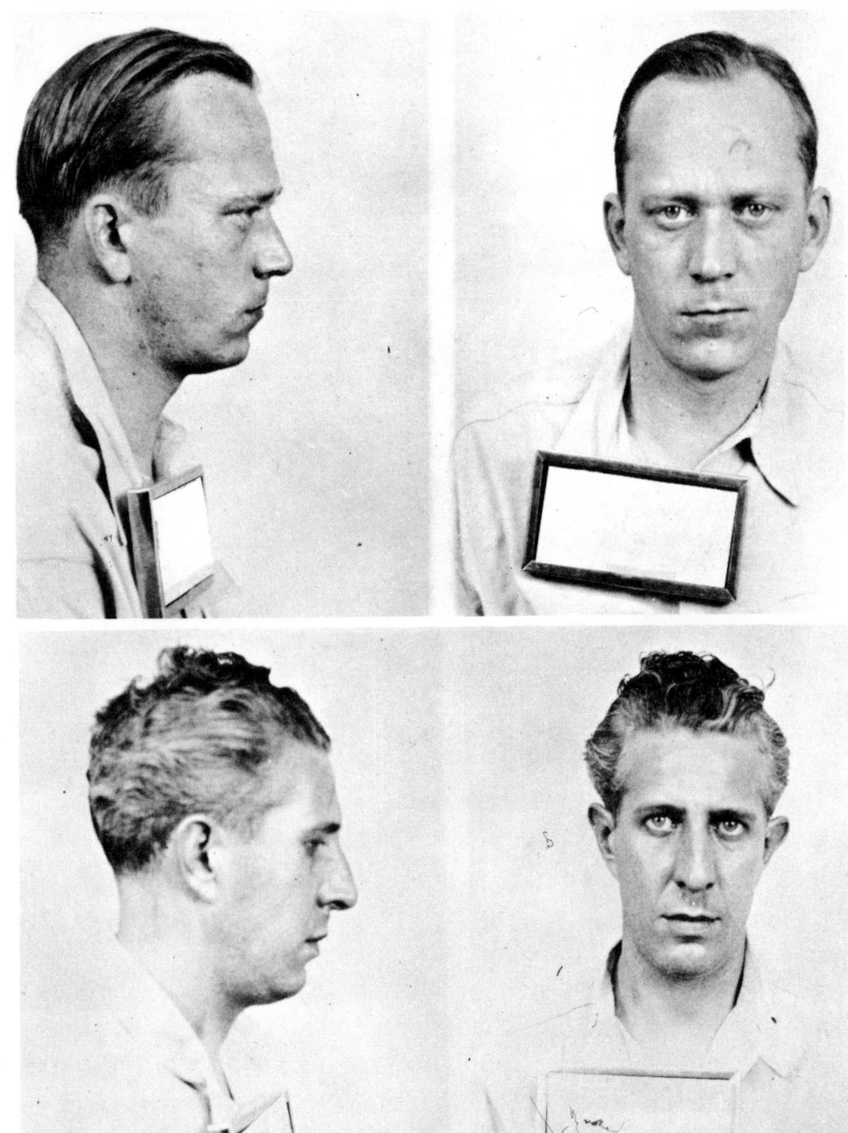

**Heinrich Harm Heinck.**

**Richard Quirin.**

they found footprints leading into the dunes. They also found the uniforms and the boxes buried in the sand. They carried their find to the Amagansett station from where it was rushed into New York to the office of Coast Guard Captain J. S. Bayliss. The Captain called in FBI agents and turned the investigation over to them.

Hoover notified President Roosevelt and the Attorney General that saboteurs had landed on Long Island. An alert was sent to all FBI offices. But at this time no one knew that another team of saboteurs was soon to land safely on the beach near Ponte Vedra, Florida.

Edward Kerling and his three men came ashore just before dawn on June 17. They buried their equipment near the beach and, about noon, caught a bus into Jacksonville. Kerling and Thiel headed for New York by way of Cincin-

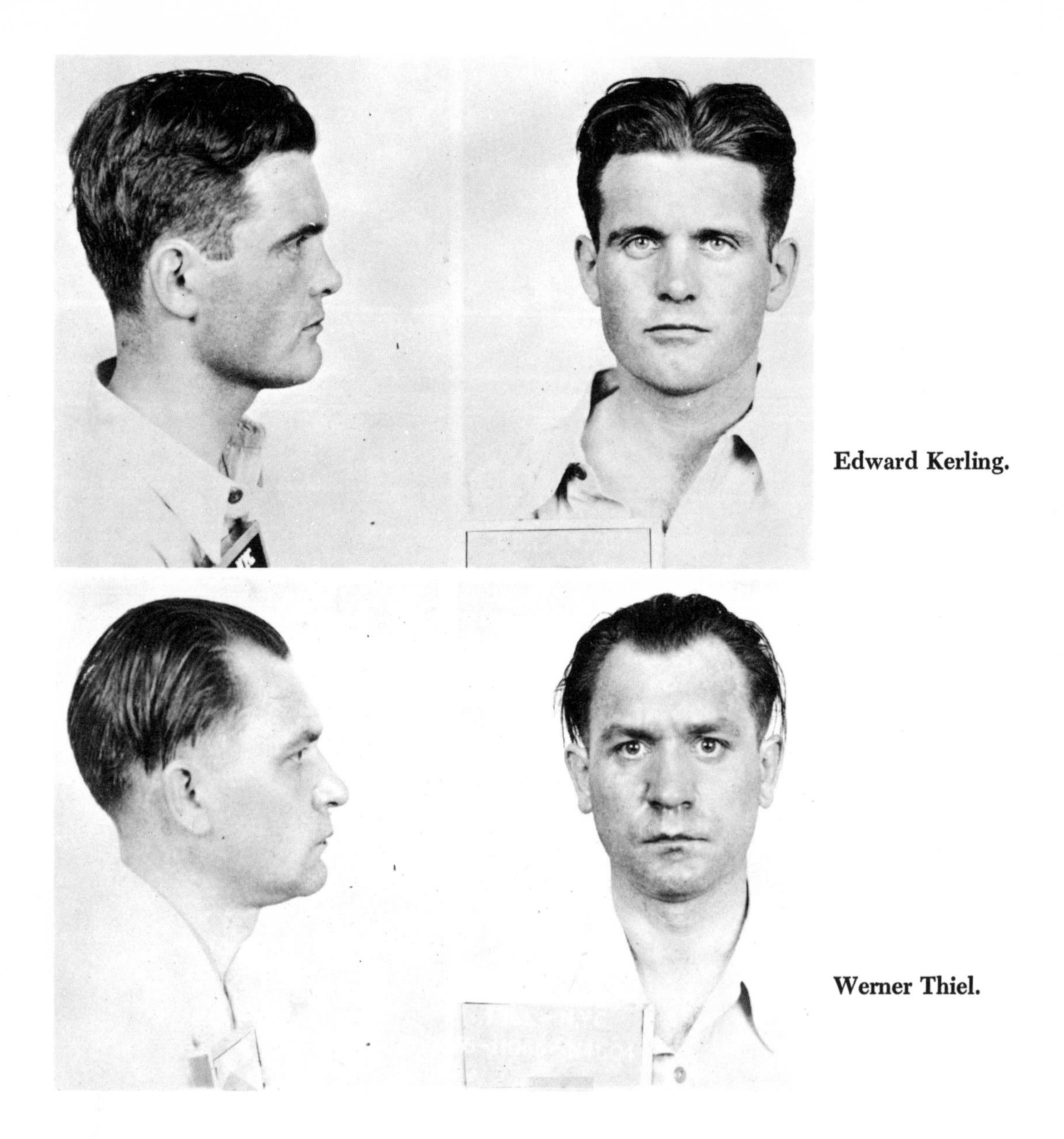

**Edward Kerling.**

**Werner Thiel.**

nati while Haupt and Neubauer took a train to Chicago. They aroused the suspicion of no one.

The Abwehr chiefs would have been dismayed, however, had they been able to listen to Dasch and Burger talking the day after their landing. They met in Dasch's room at the Governor Clinton. They knew that death could be the penalty for espionage and sabotage in time of war. They also knew the chances were that the young Coast Guardsman had reported what he saw on the beach. The scheme wasn't as exciting now as it had seemed when they were training for it.

At last Dasch said to Burger: "I'm going to notify the FBI. I'm going to Washington and tell them everything." Burger nodded. He was ready to throw in the sponge, too.

The next day an agent on duty in the New York FBI office received a call from a man who said: "I am Franz Daniel Pastorious. I want you to know that I shall get in touch with your Washington office next Thursday or Friday. I have some important information."

Before the agent could ask questions, the caller hung up. It sounded to the agent like another call from an eccentric, but he made a note of it for the record.

The next Friday at 10 A.M., a man who gave his name as Pastorious called the Bureau in Washington and asked to speak to Director Hoover.

"I am the man who called your New York office last Sunday," he said. "My real name is George John Dasch. I have just arrived from Germany with some important information. I am in room 351 at the Mayflower Hotel."

Two agents brought Dasch from his hotel room to Bureau headquarters on Pennsylvania Avenue. He told of the training at the sabotage school, the trip by submarine, and the landing on Long Island. He also told of the plan to land one team in Florida and he gave agents information concerning all the men. He handed over a handkerchief on which were written in invisible ink the names of people he was to contact.

Agents followed Burger on his trips about New York until he led them to Heinck and Quirin. Kerling and Thiel were arrested when they got in touch with a man whose name was on Dasch's handkerchief. Neubauer was picked up in Chicago where he was using the name H. Nicholas.

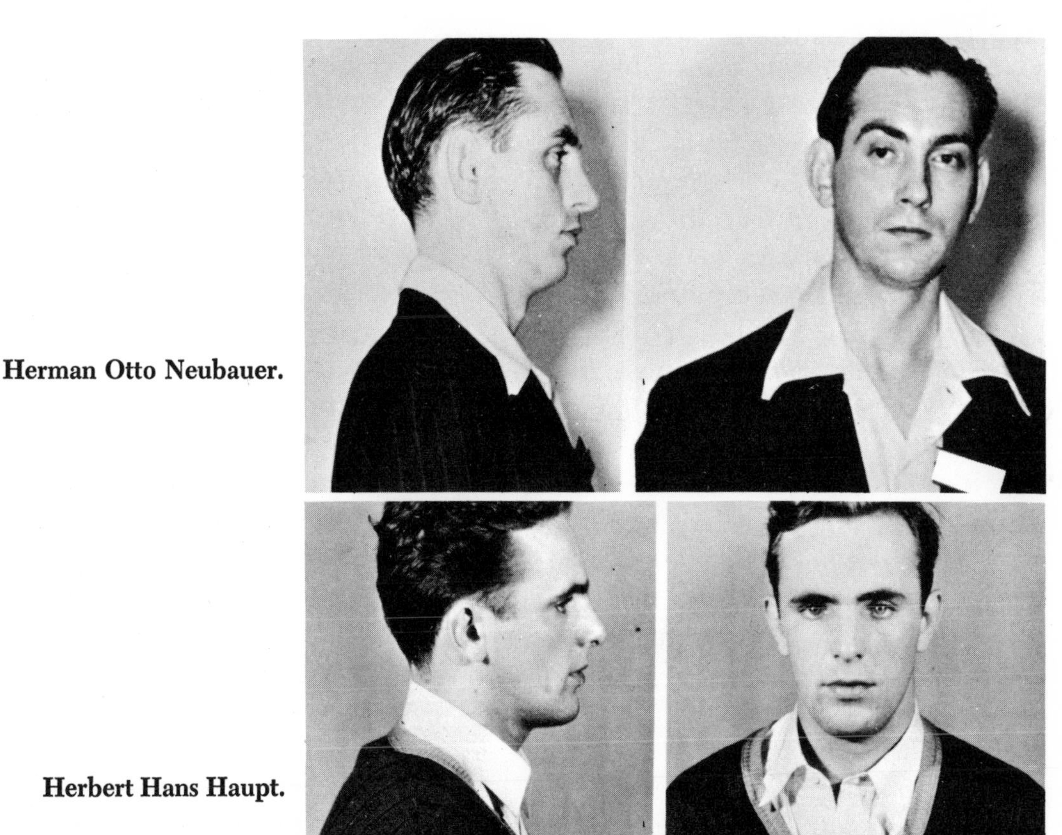

**Herman Otto Neubauer.**

**Herbert Hans Haupt.**

The last member of the saboteur teams was arrested just fourteen days after the hunt began. They had spent only $611.38 of the $175,200 bankroll given to them at the submarine base in Lorient.

President Roosevelt decided the news of the capture should be given to the newspapers at once so that it would reach Germany and perhaps discourage the Nazis from sending other teams into the country. Hoover's announcement of the roundup made sensational headlines.

When news of the capture reached Germany, Admiral Doenitz was furious. He had risked two of his submarines by sending them to the edge of the American beaches. And then his U-boats had hardly had time to return to their bases before all of the Abwehr's agents were in the hands of the enemy's FBI. He stormed that never again would he do such a foolish thing for the Abwehr.

But after the Americans and their Allies landed on the beaches of Normandy in 1944 and then drove on into the edge of Germany, Doenitz agreed to try it once more. This time a submarine landed two spies on a beach near Crab Tree Point, Maine, on November 29.

The agents were Erich Gimpel, a radio expert, and William Curtis Colepaugh, an American who had turned Nazi. They came ashore about 11 P.M. through a heavy fall of snow which seemed a bit of luck at the time. The snowstorm hid the submarine and the spies from anyone who might be watching from a lookout point.

Oddly enough, neither Gimpel nor Colepaugh wore an overcoat or a hat. In the excitement they must have left them aboard the U-boat, or lost them in the surf on landing. They walked from the beach to the highway to thumb a ride. The first car that stopped was a taxi and it took them into Bangor, Maine, a distance of about thirty-five miles. From Bangor, they went to New York City.

Several people living at Crab Tree Point had seen the two hatless, coatless strangers walking through the snow from the direction of the beach. The eighteen-year-old son of a deputy sheriff—remembering the capture of the saboteurs two years before—decided to tell the FBI about it.

The report by itself hardly seemed anything to get excited about. But on December 3—four days after the men were seen—a submarine sent a torpedo smashing into the British freighter *Cornwallis,* and it sank off the coast of Maine not far from Bangor.

Agents in the FBI's Boston office reasoned that the submarine might well have landed spies at Crab Tree Point before sinking the British ship. At least it would do no harm to look for the two strangers.

The search didn't last long. Colepaugh, like Dasch, decided he wanted no more of this game. He left Gimpel in New York and went to see a friend in Richmond Hill, New York, to whom he told his story. The friend called the FBI the day after Christmas.

Colepaugh said he didn't know where Gimpel could be found but that he had been using the name "Edward Green" the last time he saw him.

"What are some of Gimpel's habits?" an agent asked. "Does he do anything from habit that might help us find him?"

Colepaugh said Gimpel did have the habit of going to a Times Square newsstand to buy a copy of a Peruvian news-

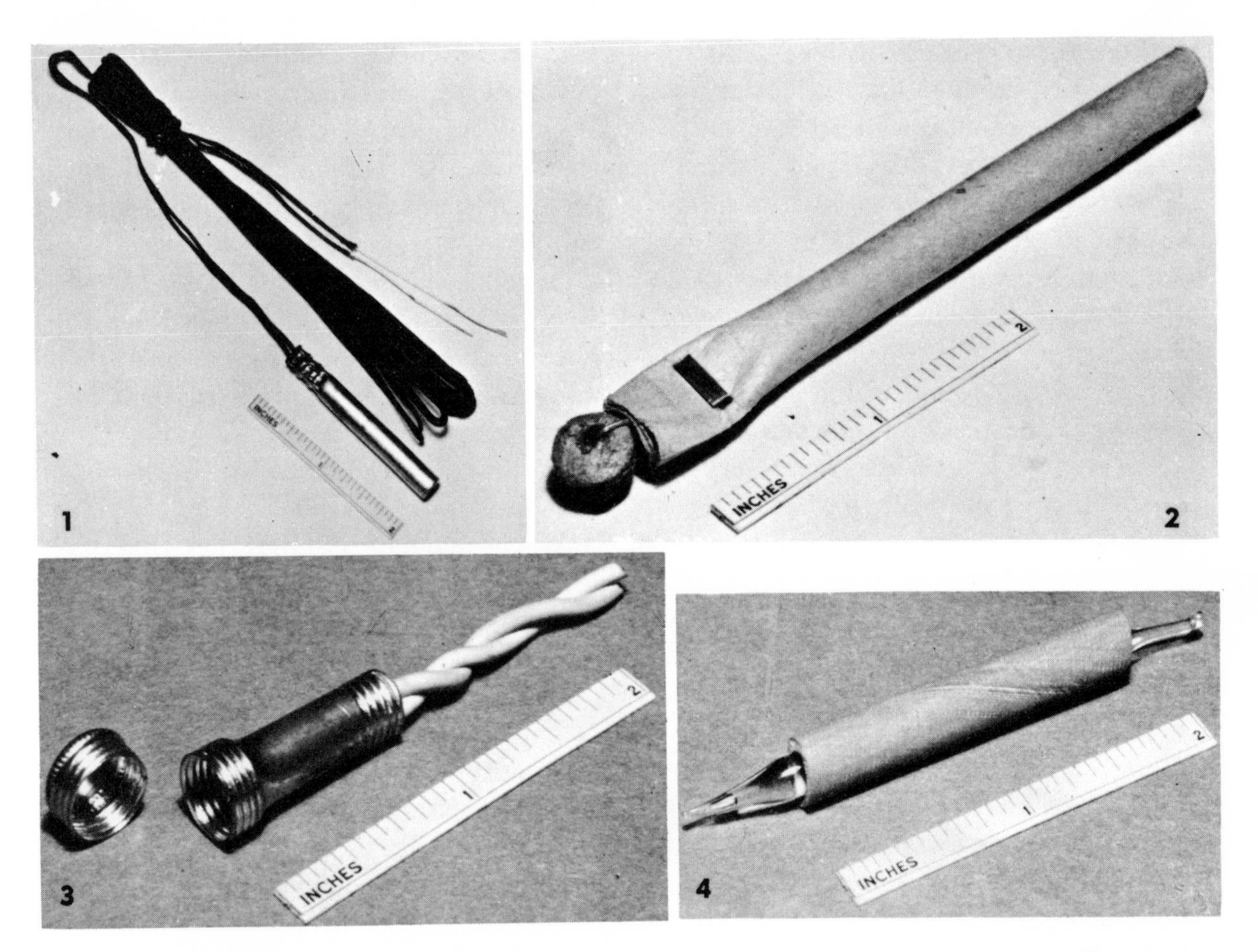


**Examples of the items of sabotage equipment recovered following arrests of the eight Nazi saboteurs:**

**1—Electric blasting cap with copper wires.**

**2—Safety fuse lighter for the ignition of standard safety fuse.**

**3—Electric match with screw cap removed—used in conjunction with timing mechanism and battery.**

**4—Capsule containing sulphuric acid encased in rubber tubing for protection.**

paper. Also, he kept his small bills in the breast pocket of his coat. That was about all he could remember.

Agents in New York started a search. They found a hotel where one guest had registered on December 22, 1944, under the name Edward Green. They watched the room for three days, but Green never did show up.

A twenty-four hour watch was placed on the Times Square newsstand. On December 30 a man who met Gimpel's description walked up and bought a magazine. He reached into the breast pocket of his coat and pulled out a bill. The agents closed in on him.

Gimpel angrily accused the agents of arresting an innocent man. He threatened to make trouble for them if they didn't let him go. But it was of no use. The agents found $10,000 in his pockets and a packet of ninety-nine small diamonds. They found another $44,000 hidden in his hotel room. And then Gimpel confessed.

It is not to be wondered at that the Nazis were angry with the Abwehr's failures in the United States. When the war ended, the Nazis' agents had not succeeded in carrying out a single act of sabotage.

Throughout the war, the FBI received many offers from people who wished to help in the fight against espionage and subversion. Some wanted to organize their own detective forces along the lines of the old American Protective League of World War I.

Movie magnate Cecil B. DeMille offered to set up an "FBI unit" in the moving picture industry. He would lead it and pay all expenses himself.

Hoover sent word to DeMille saying: "I appreciate deeply the very generous and patriotic offer . . . but at the present time it does not seem necessary . . . as we have the situation well in hand . . ."

Hoover knew the job was one for professionals and not for amateurs. He intended to keep it that way.

# 10. Danger from South of the Border

Where should the FBI be on guard to head off trouble? That's a question nobody yet has ever been able to answer. Trouble comes in so many strange places and at such unexpected times. As it did that day in Texas . . .

Continental Air Lines Flight 54 thundered from a runway at the Phoenix, Arizona, airport shortly after midnight on August 3, 1961, and climbed smoothly to 27,000 feet before leveling off for the run to El Paso, Texas.

It was a Boeing 707 Golden Jet which cruised at about 500 miles an hour with Captain Byron D. Rickards in command. At the controls with Rickards were First Officer Ralph Wagner and Second Officer Norman Simmons. Flight 54 was a regular run from Los Angeles to Houston, Texas.

The lights of Columbus, New Mexico, shone below the plane when Stewardess Lois Carnagey noticed that the small signal light had been snapped on over seats EB and EC. The seats were occupied by Leon Bearden, aged thirty-eight, and his sixteen-year-old son, Cody. They had boarded at Phoenix.

Miss Carnagey walked up the aisle and bent over the older man to hear what he was saying. "I'm sorry," she said. "What did you say?" Suddenly the passenger shoved a snub-nosed, thirty-eight caliber pistol into her side. He ordered: "Go to the cockpit."

Miss Carnagey walked toward the front of the plane with the two Beardens following. She met Stewardess Antoinette Besset in the aisle and warned her quietly: "He's got a gun."

The Beardens forced the two girls through the cockpit door and closed it behind them. Captain Rickards glanced around from the radio he was operating and saw the two passengers standing behind the stewardesses.

"They've got guns!" Miss Carnagey exclaimed. Leon Bearden held his revolver on the crewmen while Cody Bearden pointed a forty-five caliber automatic pistol.

The father, an ex-convict, was a slender man, 5-feet-9, with cold gray eyes and light brown hair that was thinning on his forehead. The son was about an inch shorter and also slender of build. His eyes were hazel and his hair brown.

Leon Bearden hated the United States. He claimed that while in prison in California he had given up his United States citizenship. He looked on Cuba's Fidel Castro as a hero. He wanted to take his son with him to Cuba where they would work with the Communists.

Bearden told the crew: "Don't get excited and nobody will get hurt. Turn this plane forty-five degrees and head for Monterey, Mexico."

Rickards protested there wasn't enough fuel in the tanks to fly to Monterey. Second Officer Simmons pointed to the gauges. "Look for yourself," he said. "We haven't got enough to go anywhere but to El Paso."

Bearden knew enough of planes to see that the officers were telling the truth.

"All right," he said. "You'll land at El Paso and take on enough fuel to fly to Cuba."

By this time the airport tower at El Paso was calling Flight 54, trying to give the plane clearance to land. The normal reply to such a call was for the plane's captain to repeat the tower's clearance word for word.

Bearden heard the tower's call and said· "Just tell 'em okay—that's all." He wanted no warning given that would bring law enforcement officers to the airport.

First Officer Wagner explained to Bearden (the father did all the talking for himself and his son) that he would have to radio the tower and tell them what had happened if he was to get any fuel. Even if he said nothing, the airport people would know something was wrong as soon as the plane landed and no one was permitted to leave the ship.

Bearden told him to go ahead—but to warn the tower that somebody would be killed or wounded if lawmen tried to stop him. Wagner then radioed the tower that the plane was in control of gunmen. It was landing only to take on fuel. He repeated Bearden's warning.

The huge jet landed at 2:10 A.M. Eight minutes later it came to a stop at its parking spot and the engines were cut. Bearden permitted Miss Carnagey to return to the main cabin to check the passengers and keep them in their seats.

The crew began to stall for time. Wagner argued that the crew had never flown to Cuba, they didn't know the distance, and they had no maps to guide them. He said such a flight would be impossible unless the crew could talk it over with company officials.

Bearden agreed but he added, "Lay off the map kick." He said all the passengers had to remain in their seats. No doors were to be opened and no one was to come near the plane from the outside.

"How much fuel will you need to reach Cuba?" Bearden asked. "And how long will it take to load it?"

He was told they probably could reach Cuba with 90,000 pounds of fuel which could be loaded in about an hour.

"Tell 'em to get going," Bearden ordered. His order was relayed to the tower.

Miss Carnagey, as calmly as possible, told the passengers what was happening. When a pregnant woman began to sob, Miss Carnagey set her jaw and returned to the cockpit to plead with the Beardens to let the woman off the plane.

Bearden snapped, "No!" But the stewardess continued her pleading. At last Bearden said all right—all the passengers except four could leave the plane. They were to remain as his prisoners along with the crewmen and the stewardesses until the plane reached Cuba.

When this word was passed on to the passengers, four men quickly volunteered to stay behind. They were John Casey, a Continental Air Lines employee; Truman Cleveland, an Army enlisted man; Leonard W. Gilman of the U. S. Border Patrol; and Luis L. Erives. Louis Finch, director of passenger service for Continental Air Lines, also remained aboard the plane with the other five Continental employees. They sat with the guns of the Beardens leveled at them while the passengers filed off, and then the door of the plane was slammed shut again.

News of the hijacking already was flashing across the country. As soon as the tower learned that gunmen had seized the plane, Continental Air Lines officials called the FBI and other law enforcement agencies. Armed men raced to the airport from the FBI, El Paso police, sheriff's office, Texas Department of Public Safety, Customs Agency Service, Secret Service, and other agencies.

A command post was set up in the airport under the direction of FBI Special Agent in Charge Francis Crosby of El Paso. Orders came from Washington: Do everything possible to protect the hostages—but do not permit the plane to leave El Paso.

The officers waited for something to happen . . . anything . . . that would lead to the capture of the gunmen without danger to the lives of the men and women held at gun point. At this time no one outside knew how many armed men were trying to hijack the plane. At first the crew had thought there were four men in the plot.

The re-fueling dragged on but the wing tanks finally were full. It was about 6:30 A.M. and the plane had been on the ground for more than four hours. Prodded by Bearden's threats, Captain Rickards asked the tower for clearance to take off. He was told not to leave.

"The whole thing is out of our hands now," the tower said. "It's in the hands of the government."

"It's out of our hands, too," Rickards said dryly. "We're in worse trouble than you and we are going."

Hurried plans were made inside the airport. Several officers raced to the cover of a building near Runway 4. Then the tower passed along the word that Rickards could move the plane to Runway 4 for take-off.

The tower asked for the names of all the hostages. Bearden told Rickards: "Tell them we will issue a statement when we are in the air for the benefit of the U. S. Government and the people."

The plane taxied slowly to the end of the runway. The high-pitched whine of the jet engines grew louder and the huge ship began to move down the runway. It had moved only a few yards when seven automobiles loaded with armed men raced from a nearby building. They opened fire and the hail of bullets punctured the plane's big balloon tires. The jet jolted to a halt and Rickards cut the engines.

Inside the cockpit, Leon Bearden placed his gun to the head of Miss Carnagey. He held it there for five minutes as though trying to decide whether to pull the trigger. Then he lowered the gun.

The plane was now surrounded by officers. The hot morning sun was beating on the aluminum shell of the ship and the temperature climbed inside the cabin.

Someone outside connected the plane once more to the airport's ground communication system. Crosby asked to speak to the hijackers. He told Bearden he was an FBI agent and for him to listen closely to what he had to say.

"This plane is not going to leave the ground," he said. He told him of the orders received from Washington and the senseless position the hijackers were now in. They were going to be prosecuted. No deals would be made. If any harm came to anyone aboard the plane, they would be in deeper trouble. He asked to be let aboard to talk things over.

Bearden agreed and in the confusion of getting Crosby into the plane, Louis Finch and the stewardesses, two crew-

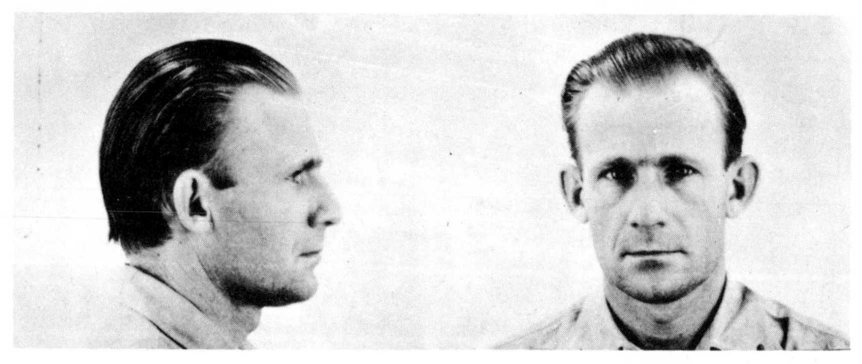

Leon Bearden.

men, and three of the hostages escaped from a rear hatchway.

Crosby found Leon and Cody Bearden in the forward lounge of the airliner with Border Patrolman Gilman and Second Officer Simmons. Gilman and Simmons were in the aisle. Cody Bearden sat in a window seat next to his father who faced the door to the pilot's cabin.

Crosby urged the father and son to surrender, and asked why they had done this thing.

Leon Bearden said he didn't want to live any longer in the United States. He didn't have the money to buy passage to Cuba for his wife and four children—so he planned to hijack the ship, fly to Cuba with his oldest boy, and then send for the other members of the family.

The men talked in the lounge of the plane for almost an hour. About 11:50 A.M. a rap came on the cockpit door. Simmons cracked open the door and then shut it quickly. Crosby and Gilman realized that other officers had slipped into the pilot's cabin through a hatchway. They glanced at each other.

Suddenly Gilman crashed his fist into Leon Bearden's jaw and pinned his arms. Crosby lunged for Cody Bearden and yanked him out of his seat. A Border Patrolman and an FBI agent rushed through the cockpit door.

The morning of terror was over.

Leon Bearden received a long prison sentence. His son was ordered imprisoned until he was twenty-one years old.

Fidel Castro's government had no part in the plot to hijack the plane. But the case was a clear warning to the FBI that anything might happen as long as the Communists held a base so near the United States. The need to be on guard was underscored in November, 1962, when FBI agents found evidence that five Castro agents were plotting a campaign of sabotage with gasoline refineries and large department stores as targets. Three of them were members of the Cuban Mission to the United Nations.

Agents kept a watch on the suspects for days before making their move. Then they raided a workshop run by a pro-Castro Cuban on West 27th Street and found hand grenades, fire bombs, and other items used for sabotage and for guerrilla warfare. The ring was broken up.

The trouble caused directly and indirectly by the fall of Cuba to the Communists reminded many of the FBI's old-time agents of the days in World War II when there was trouble "south of the Border." This was when they set out to break up Nazi spy rings operating in

Central and South America.

For more than sixteen years this amazing adventure was kept secret. It began in 1940 when President Roosevelt and others in the government received proof that the Nazis had set up a network of spy bases from Mexico City to the southern tip of South America. Their agents were being sent from Germany into South America and then into the United States.

Roosevelt gave the FBI the go-ahead on a plan to organize a Special Intelligence Service (SIS) to fight the threat. Within thirty days FBI agents were moving south as soap salesmen, engineers, stockbrokers, and businessmen looking for orders. Later, a few went to work in American Embassies or were stationed as liaison officers with police forces in other countries, with approval of the governments involved.

One young agent—we'll call him George Stevens—went into Argentina under cover of being a reporter for an American newspaper. He joined the clubs to which other reporters belonged and went about his job of gathering and sending news just as any newsman would.

Stevens' favorite hangout was a hotel run by a man whose parents still lived

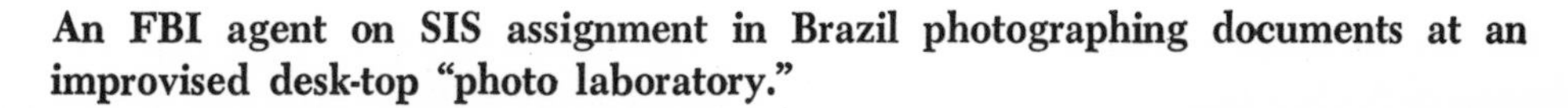

**An FBI agent on SIS assignment in Brazil photographing documents at an improvised desk-top "photo laboratory."**

in a country which had been seized by the Nazis. They had tried to force him to become a spy for them, but he had refused.

Stevens talked whenever he could with the innkeeper because the man always seemed to know what was going on in the city. He was the leader in a club which had members in every important government and business office. If anyone could help uncover the Nazi spies, this man could.

One day, over a cup of coffee, Stevens said to the innkeeper: "I'd like to do a series of stories and I'd like your help in gathering the information."

The man looked at Stevens and said: "If I give you this information, will it reach the right people?" He knew Stevens was asking him to help spy on the Germans.

"Yes," Stevens said, "and I promise you'll never be embarrassed."

From that day on, the innkeeper fed information to Stevens. Not only did he report what the Germans were doing, but often what they were saying. One report made on two Germans helped uncover a spy ring.

"Would you mind telling me how you got the report?" Stevens asked later.

The innkeeper smiled. "The man who drove their car was one of my men. When those people ask for a car in this city, the driver is always my man."

Slowly SIS agents learned that the Nazi spy rings were operating mostly in Brazil, Argentina, Chile and Mexico. They sat for long hours at radios listening for broadcasts made from secret radio stations. They followed the trails of Germans into the jungle country and up the Amazon river. They searched the coasts for places which U-boats might possibly be using as bases.

One of the cleverest of the Nazi recruits was Josef Jacob Johannes Starziczny who was both an engineer and a scientist. He was trained in espionage in Germany in 1940 and then sent to Brazil in 1941.

Starziczny was a small man who wore thick glasses. He arrived in Rio de Janeiro aboard the SS *Hermes* booked as Niels Christian Christensen, a citizen of Denmark. With the aid of confederates, he smuggled ashore a black leather bag in which he carried a radio transmitter, code books, and micro-dot messages. Soon he was sending radio messages back to Germany, using the call letters CIT.

Starziczny had orders from his Abwehr bosses never to keep notes or messages that might fall into the hands of enemies. But the little man liked to save things and to tuck them away in desks and drawers in neat files.

He made his first serious mistake when he went to Santos, Brazil, to set up a radio transmitter and found he needed a wave meter. He went to a radio shop and tried to buy the part.

"I don't have one in stock," the shopkeeper said, "but if you will leave your name and address, I shall forward it to you." Starziczny wrote on a piece of paper, "O. Mendes, Hotel Santos, Santos."

The shopkeeper remembered his government's warning that radios and radio parts should not be sold to strangers. He called the police and told them what had happened. He gave them the name and address on the slip of paper.

The police, working with SIS agents, began checking on the names of all persons who had bought radio wave meters

These two pictures show the removal of a box containing $55,000 in U. S. currency which had been buried in the garden of a leader of German espionage operations in Chile. More than $200,000 in U. S. currency had been given to this spy by an official of the German Embassy at Santiago, Chile, in 1943.

**Josef Jacob Johannes Starziczny.**

in past months. The trail finally led to "Christensen" whose real name, they learned, was Starziczny.

The man's habit of saving letters and messages was a stroke of luck for the SIS agents and the police. In his desk and bank deposit box they found code books and messages along with the names of other agents.

Among the papers, too, was evidence that Starziczny was the man who once had given the Nazis information which threatened the lives of 10,000 troops and placed the huge British liner, the *Queen Mary,* in grave danger.

The big luxury liner—then being used as a troop carrier—arrived in Rio de Janeiro on March 6, 1942, jammed with troops on their way to England. An FBI radio monitoring station picked up a message from the secret Nazi station CIT which said: "*Queen Mary* arrived here today at 10:00 . . . She must (go) to the cellar."

Two days later another hidden radio messaged: "*Queen Mary* sailed on March 8 at 18 o'clock local time." And next day the CIT operator said: "With *Queen Mary* falls Churchill . . . Good luck . . ."

The sea raiders were alerted by these messages that the ship was at sea. She was traveling alone without even a single destroyer to protect her.

These messages intercepted by the FBI were passed along to the British.

One week later the Italian radio broadcast a report which said: "In Argentine maritime circles it is affirmed that the British transatlantic (liner) *Queen Mary,* which left Rio de Janeiro a few days ago with 10,000 North American troops aboard headed for an unknown destination, was torpedoed. The ship was damaged heavily and tried to reach the British base at Falkland Islands . . ."

But the report was false. The *Queen Mary* brought the troops safely into port.

The agents with the most dangerous jobs were those who were sent into Argentina. The government of President Pedro Ramirez was anti-American and SIS agents lived in danger of being arrested and perhaps tortured.

Early in 1944 Ramirez's police picked up several Argentinians who had been working secretly with the SIS. Their arrest threatened the entire operation. An FBI inspector sent an urgent message to Hoover saying: "I am . . . concerned with the tremendous danger of one of our agents being picked up in Argentina, tortured into a full confession . . . I do not think we can ignore overwhelming evidence which we have to the effect that the German agents are working hand-in-hand with the present Argentine regime . . ."

**These pictures show transmitting, receiving and other radio equipment located on the premises of a German citizen who was recruited into a Nazi espionage network in South America in 1943.**

Hoover decided the five agents in Argentina should be brought out of the country. He sent orders for them to move quickly into friendly countries.

A short time later a coded message came from Buenos Aires saying:

> Reference your radiogram 772, all necessary preparations now under way for early departure of 241, 243, 582, 361, and 363 to Montevideo . . .

Under cover of darkness, these men slipped out of Buenos Aires in a boat which had been hidden on the waterfront and kept in readiness for just such a crisis. They moved across the Rio de la Plata into friendly Uruguay. But later there would be other agents to take their places.

When the war ended, the SIS was disbanded. The agents were brought home because intelligence work outside the United States was being turned over to a central agency despite protests from many in the government that the FBI should remain on the job.

But the FBI's work of searching for spies wasn't finished. In fact, it was only beginning.

# 11. The Hollow Nickel Spy Case

It isn't often a thirteen-year-old boy plays a part in helping capture a spy. But that's what Jimmy Bozart did when he found a hollowed-out nickel in his pocket one Monday evening in June, 1953. This five-cent piece gave warning to the FBI that a Soviet spy was loose somewhere in the United States.

It all began that warm evening in Brooklyn, New York, when Jimmy left home after supper to collect from some of his newspaper customers. Each day he carried the Brooklyn *Eagle* to subscribers in his neighborhood and periodically he settled up his accounts.

He was making the usual rounds when he knocked on a door in the apartment building at 3403 Foster Avenue. The woman who opened the door smiled when she saw Jimmy. "I'll bet you want some money," she said.

"Yes, ma'am," Jimmy said.

The woman left him at the door and returned in a moment with her purse. "Sorry, Jimmy," she said. "I don't have any change. Can you break this dollar for me?"

Jimmy counted the coins in his pocket and shook his head. "I'll ask the people across the hall," he said. "Maybe they can."

The two women who lived in the opposite apartment searched through their purses. Between them they found the change for a dollar. And Jimmy went on his way.

He walked along jingling the coins in his hand. He noticed that one of them had a dead sound to it, as though it might be a slug. He picked out a nickel and placed it on the end of his middle finger. It felt lighter than the other nickels. Then the nickel slipped off his finger and broke apart at his feet. He picked up the pieces and saw a tiny photograph inside one of the halves. It looked as though someone had taken a picture of nothing but rows of numbers.

The next day Jimmy told a girl friend about the hollow nickel with the photograph inside. She told the tale to her father, a policeman, and he mentioned the story to Detective Frank R. Milley of the New York City Police Department.

It wasn't the finding of a hollow nickel which interested the detective so much as the report of the picture inside. Milley got Jimmy to give him the nickel and the picture, and he turned them over to an FBI agent.

When agents in the New York FBI office placed the picture under a magnifying glass, they counted ten columns of five-digit numbers. Most of the columns had twenty-one numbers. They suspected the numbers were an espionage code of some kind. Soviet agents often hid their messages in hollow cuff links, pencils, and the like.

The nickel and micro-photograph were sent to the FBI Laboratory experts in Washington for a closer study. They had seen trick coins before, but never one quite like this. The "heads" side of the coin was a 1948 Jefferson nickel. The "tails" side was made from a nickel minted sometime between 1942 and 1945—the years when the government was using a copper-silver alloy because of a war-time shortage of nickel. A tiny hole had been drilled in the letter "R" of the word "TRUST" so that a pin or needle could be pushed through to force the coin apart.

The picture was turned over to experts on codes to see if they could find the key to any message that might be hidden in the numbers.

In Brooklyn, special agents talked to Jimmy Bozart and he told them how he had obtained the nickel. They talked to the women who had given the boy change for a dollar and showed them photographs of the hollow coin.

"Do you remember having a coin like this?" an agent asked.

The women shook their heads. One of them said: "We've never seen a hollow coin or even heard of one before." If it had been in their purse that night, they hadn't noticed it.

Agents visited stores in New York which sold novelties and supplies to amateur and professional magicians. None of the store owners had ever seen a coin of that type. One salesman said: "It's not suitable for a magic trick. The hollowed-out area is too small to hide anything other than a tiny piece of paper. Nobody could even see anything that small from an audience."

The FBI's experts were not able to break the code. But they knew the numbers had been written on a foreign-made typewriter because the type-face did not match the type used on American machines.

The search for the person who had passed the hollow nickel spread across the United States. Agents turned up hollow pennies, subway tokens, and

**The hollowed-out nickel that led the FBI to a Soviet spy.**

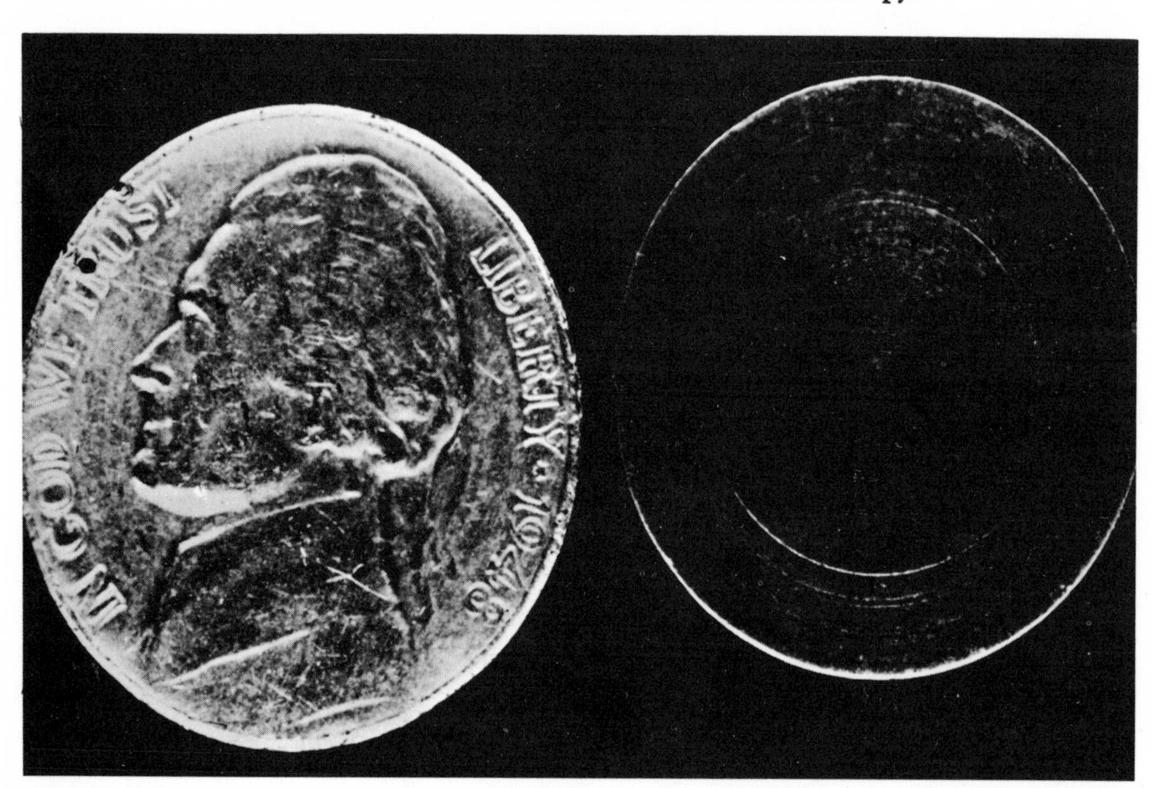

other metal objects which looked like coins. A hollowed-out half dollar was found in New York. But none had been made in the same way as Jimmy Bozart's nickel.

For four years, agents kept the coin in mind whenever they talked to anyone who might know something about it. Many Soviet intelligence agents who escaped to the West from behind the Iron Curtain were questioned about the nickel and the picture. None could give the agents any help.

The break came in May, 1957, when a man walked into the United States Embassy in Paris, France. He told an Embassy official: "I am an officer in the Soviet intelligence service. For the past five years I have been operating in the United States. Now I need your help."

He pulled from his pocket an American passport which identified him as Eugene Nicolai Maki, born May 30, 1919, in Enaville, Idaho. But he said his real name was Reino Hayhanen and that he was a lieutenant colonel in the Soviet State Security Service (KGB). Five years earlier the Soviets had sent him to the United States on an espionage mission. In April, 1957, Moscow had ordered him to return home. But he was afraid—and after five years of living in the United States he wanted no part of life in Soviet Russia.

Hayhanen told a strange tale of having been given the name of another man and then being sent to the United States as a spy . . .

He was the son of Russian peasants. He had been an honor student and, following graduation from a teachers college near Leningrad in June of 1939, had started a career in teaching. Then war broke out in Europe. On November 29, 1939, he was drafted into the Soviet secret police. Because he spoke Finnish fluently, he was sent to the Russian-Finnish war front to translate captured documents and to question prisoners of war. He became a member of the Communist Party and rose to the rank of senior agent in Intelligence.

In the summer of 1948, Moscow ordered Hayhanen into Estonia to begin a more important assignment. During the day he worked as a mechanic. At night and on his days off he studied to be a spy. Then at the end of a year he was sent into Finland with papers which identified him as Eugene Nicolai Maki, an American-born laborer.

There had been a real Eugene Nicolai Maki born in Enaville, Idaho. His mother was an American married to an emigrant from Finland. The Makis had left Enaville in the mid-1920s to make their home in Russia. They wrote friends from time to time—unhappy letters which made it clear they had not found the "New Russia" they had been led to believe they would find.

Gradually the letters stopped. As the years passed, only two or three people were left in Enaville who remembered a family named Maki or that they had a son.

For three years, Hayhanen lived in Finland as Eugene Maki. He worked hard. He fell in love with Hanna Kurikka and they were married. But even Hanna did not know his real name. He kept his secret well as he waited for orders from Moscow.

At last the orders came and on July 3, 1951, Eugene Maki went to the American Embassy in Helsinki to ask for a passport. He handed over a birth certificate from the State of Idaho showing he was born in Enaville on May 30, 1919. He told the Vice Consul of being brought to Russia as a child. He signed an affidavit saying:

> I accompanied my mother to Estonia when I was eight years of age and resided with her until her death in 1941. I left Estonia for Finland in June, 1943, and have resided here for the reason that I have no funds with which to pay my transportation to the United States.

Hayhanen waited another year. On July 28, 1952, he was issued an American passport at Helsinki. Then he slipped back to Moscow where he was introduced to the man who would direct his espionage work in the United States —an agent he would know only as Mikhail.

A Soviet official told Hayhanen that when he arrived in New York, he must go to the Tavern on the Green in Central Park. Nearby he would find a signpost marked "Horse Carts."

"You will let Mikhail know of your arrival by placing a red thumbtack in this signpost," the official said. "If you suspect you are being watched, place a white thumbtack on the board."

Hayhanen returned to Finland from this meeting and began to arrange for his trip to the United States. He and his wife agreed that she should wait for four months and then follow him.

"Eugene Maki" arrived in New York aboard the *Queen Mary* on October 21, 1952. After a short time he went to Central Park and placed the red thumbtack in the sign near the Tavern on the Green. Once again he met Mikhail who gave him his assignments. They worked together for nearly two years. Then Mikhail disappeared and Hayhanen was turned over to another Soviet agent he knew only as "Mark."

This was the story Hayhanen told in Paris in May, 1957. Every detail was checked carefully. When there was no doubt he was telling the truth, he was brought back to the United States.

FBI agents questioned Hayhanen for hours. He said he and Mikhail met only when necessary at the Prospect Park subway station. Most of the time they exchanged messages by leaving them in "dead drops" such as the base of a light post in Fort Tryon Park or a picket fence at the end of Seventh Avenue near Macombs Bridge. One spot they used was a hole in cement steps in Prospect Park.

Agents went to the steps and found where a hole had been filled with cement at some time when the steps were being repaired. The cement was dug out and they uncovered a bolt about two inches long and one-fourth inch in diameter.

The bolt was hollow. Inside was a typewritten message which said:

> Nobody came to meeting either 8 or 9th . . . as I was advised he should. Why? Should he be inside or outside? Is time wrong? Place seems right. Please check.

Hayhanen said the trick bolt was one of the devices Soviet agents often used. Sometimes the bolts were magnetized so they could be stuck to anything made of metal.

Agents searched Hayhanen's home in Peekskill, New York. Among other things they found a small Finnish coin which had been hollowed out in the same fashion as the nickel which had

**Fort Tryon Park. The opening at the base of the lamppost was used as a Soviet espionage "drop."**

been discovered by Jimmy Bozart. It also had a tiny hole in it for opening the coin. The FBI Laboratory was certain the Finnish coin and Jimmy Bozart's nickel came from the same source.

Hayhanen was questioned about the codes he used as a Soviet agent. He told as much as he could remember. It was all the FBI needed to break the code hidden in the nickel. The message read:

1. We congratulate you on a safe arrival. We confirm the receipt of your letter to the address 'V repeat V' and the reading of letter Number 1.
2. For organization of cover, we gave instructions to transmit to you three thousand in local (currency). Consult with us prior to investing it in any kind of business, advising the character of this business.
3. According to your request, we will transmit the formula for the preparation of soft film and news separately, together with (your) mother's letter.
4. It is too early to send you the *gammas*. Encipher short letters, but the longer ones make with insertions. All the data about yourself, place or work, address, etc., must not be transmitted in one cipher message. Transmit insertions separately.
5. The package was delivered to your wife personally. Everything is all right with the family. We wish you success. Greetings from the comrades. Number 1, 3rd of December.

But who was Mikhail, the man to whom Hayhanen reported when he first arrived in the United States? The description given by Hayhanen matched very closely that of Mikhail Nikolaevich Svirin who once had been First Secretary to the Soviet delegation to the United Nations.

Agents showed Hayhanen a batch of photographs. He looked through them and then pointed to one and said: "That's the man. There is absolutely no doubt about it. That's Mikhail." It was a photograph of Svirin, who had returned to the Soviet Union in 1956.

The problem now was to find the mysterious "Mark" who had taken over from Mikhail and probably was still in the United States as a spy. Hayhanen said he had received a message in 1954 telling him to go to a movie theater in Flushing, Long Island. He was to wear a blue and red striped tie and smoke a pipe. That was how he met Mark.

He knew Mark held the rank of colonel in the Soviet State Security Service and had been in espionage work since 1927. He had entered the United States illegally in 1948 or 1949 by crossing the border from Canada.

"Mark was about fifty years old or perhaps older," Hayhanen said. "He was, I would say, five-feet-ten-inches tall and medium size. He had thin gray hair." Also, he added, Mark was very good at photography.

He recalled that one day in 1955, Mark had taken him to a storage room where he kept photo supplies. The room was on the fourth or fifth floor of a building near Clark and Fulton Streets in Brooklyn.

Agents at once began to search for the storage room. They found that a man named Emil R. Goldfus had a photographic studio on the fifth floor of a building at 252 Fulton Street. At one time he also had rented a storage room on the same floor.

But Goldfus was not to be found.

Someone remembered hearing Goldfus say he was going South on a seven-weeks vacation. "It's doctor's orders," he had said. "I have a sinus condition." (This was about the time that Moscow had ordered Hayhanen to return to Russia.)

The descriptions of Goldfus given by people in the neighborhood fitted Hayhanen's description of Mark. Agents began a twenty-four hour watch on the building.

For two weeks they looked over everyone who entered or came near the building. On May 28, 1957, they saw a man who resembled Mark sitting on a bench in a park across the street from the entrance to the Fulton Street building. From time to time he would leave the bench and walk around the park, looking about nervously.

At 6:50 P.M., the man began walking from the park. The agent in charge of the surveillance passed the word: "Don't follow him. We can't be sure he's the man. If that is Mark, he'll be back."

Sixteen more days passed with no sign of Emil Goldfus. The watch continued unbroken. Then at 10:00 P.M. on June 13, the agents saw lights go on in the Goldfus studio and they caught glimpses of a man walking about the room. The lights went off at 11:52 P.M. and a few minutes later a man left the building.

Agents trailed him to a subway station. They were following him when he walked out of the subway in Manhattan and went to a room at the Hotel Latham on East 28th Street. The room was registered to "Martin Collins."

Next day agents secretly took photographs of "Collins" as he came from the hotel. The pictures were developed and taken to Hayhanen. "You've found him!" he exclaimed. "That's Mark!"

For six more days and nights agents watched every move made by Mark until all the loose ends of the investigation were tied together. He was arrested on the morning of June 21 by Immigration and Naturalization Service agents. The warrant charged illegal entry into the United States and failure to register as an alien.

Mark was defiant. But at last he admitted his real name was Rudolf Ivanovich Abel and that he had entered Canada in 1948 on a passport which belonged to a former resident of Detroit, Michigan.

He refused to talk about his espionage. But it was hardly necessary since Hayhanen was willing to testify against him. Also, there was other evidence. In his photo studio and hotel room, agents found shortwave radios; cipher pads; cameras and film for turning out microdot messages; and hollow containers such as cuff links and a shaving brush. He had two birth certificates, one in the name of Emil R. Goldfus and another in the name of Martin Collins. The FBI discovered that the real Emil R. Goldfus had died in infancy. The certificate for Martin Collins was a forgery.

Rudolf Ivanovich Abel was convicted in Federal court of espionage and sent to prison on November 15, 1957. He appealed, claiming that his rights under the Constitution and laws of the United States had been violated. The Supreme Court upheld the conviction.

Abel spent less than five years in prison. Then in February, 1962, he was turned over to the Soviets in exchange for Francis Gary Powers, an American U-2 pilot whose plane was downed

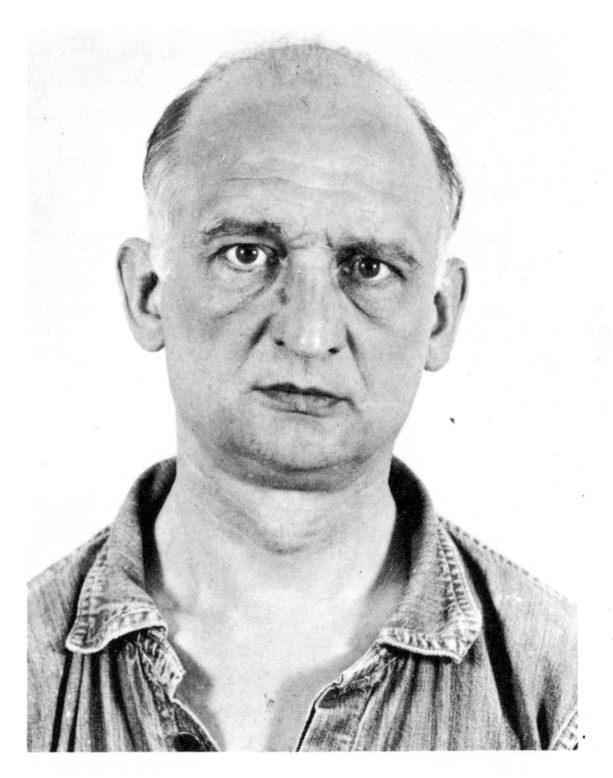

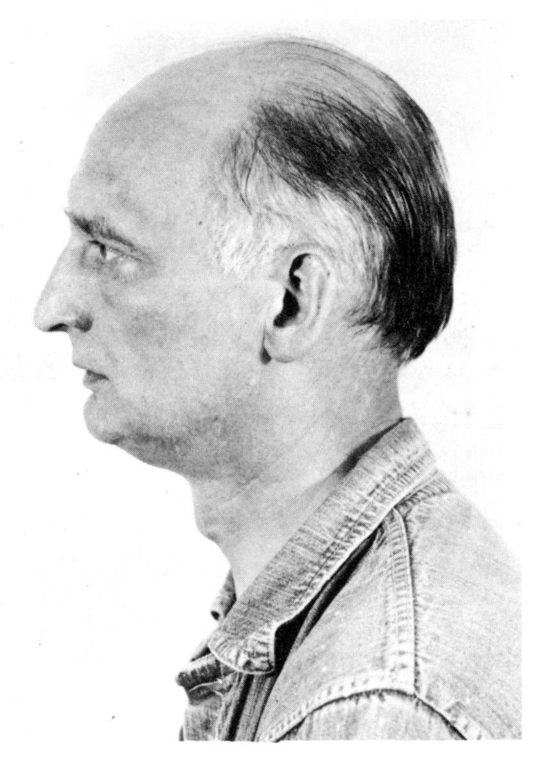

Rudolf Ivanovich Abel, 1958.

Hollow items used by Abel:

1—Carefully hollowed containers for courier transmittal of microfilmed messages to Moscow.

2—What the well-dressed spy will wear —a hollow cuff link.

over Russia while he was on a photographic mission.

The capture and conviction of Abel was only one of a long series of cases over the years in which the FBI worked to uncover Soviet spies. Time after time, the FBI turned up evidence that the Soviets were using their Embassy, the trading firm Amtorg, and their United Nations office as centers for espionage. During the ten years beginning January, 1953, and ending December, 1962, more than thirty Soviet officials were trapped in acts of espionage or related activities beyond the scope of their official duties in the United States.

The records show they were able to enlist some American citizens in their cause, as well as to transplant spies from other countries to our shores. Such a "transplant" was Dr. Robert Soble, also known as Soblen, whom the Soviets originally recruited for espionage purposes in the 1930s. Soble entered the United States in 1941 and became a naturalized citizen.

In 1961, Soble was convicted as a member of a Soviet spy ring. After appealing his conviction, he was released on $100,000 bail and subsequently fled from the United States, using the Canadian passport of his dead brother, Beras. He was arrested in Israel for illegal entry into the country.

Soble fought in the courts of Israel and then in the courts of England to block his return to the United States. When all these efforts failed, he took a fatal dose of drugs. He died in an English hospital on September 11, 1962.

One who tried to betray secrets to the Soviets was Air Force Captain George Holmes French. On April 5, 1957, he left a letter on the grounds of the Soviet Embassy in Washington, D. C., offering to sell the Russians valuable information if they would pay him $27,500. He said he could be reached at Room 1877, Hotel New Yorker, New York City.

The letter came into the hands of the FBI. The next day an FBI special agent and an Air Force investigator called on Captain French. Posing as Soviet agents, they listened to French's offer to sell the military documents he had taken from Ramey Air Force Base.

French was arrested. He admitted leaving the letter on the Soviet Embassy grounds, saying he was trying to get money to pay off gambling debts. He was tried in a military court and convicted of trying to pass classified information to the Soviets. He was dismissed from the service and sent to prison for life but the sentence was later reduced to ten years hard labor.

One Soviet effort to recruit a spy—an effort that failed—began in the summer of 1954 when a United States Army colonel stationed in West Berlin was invited to have lunch with a Soviet Air Force officer in the Red sector of East Berlin. The colonel, who was due to retire soon from the Army, accepted and subsequently also agreed to a second luncheon meeting.

The colonel drove to meet the Russian in East Berlin for a second time one rainy day in August. They went to a small, two-story house. Soon a knock came at the door and a man entered, dressed in civilian clothes. He was introduced to the colonel.

"Hello, Colonel, how are you?" the visitor said in excellent English. He talked of having lived in New York during the war, implying that he had worked at the Russian trade center known as Amtorg. He made it clear he was a Russian.

After a time the Soviet officer excused himself from the room and the visitor came quickly to the point.

"Colonel," he said, "if I come to the States, could I come and see you there?"

"Why, certainly," the American replied.

As the man continued to talk, the colonel began to realize that he was being asked to become a spy for the Soviets when he returned home. The Russian wanted him to get maps, books, and other information from the Army's Command and General Staff School at Fort Leavenworth, Kansas.

The Soviet drew a chart of downtown Manhattan and placed a dot at the northeast corner of 86th Street and Madison Avenue. He asked the colonel to meet him on any one of several dates. If he did not appear himself, one of his friends would be there.

He said: "If another must be sent, he will walk up to you and say, 'Seems to me that I have met you at Spechstrasse, Colonel. What is the number of your house there?' And you should reply, 'Oh, yes, I have lived there at Spechstrasse 19.' "

"I'll have to think it over," the colonel said. Then he made a sketch of the map drawn by the Russian and stuck it in his pocket. The Russian asked him if he needed any money to help with expenses and the colonel said no.

When he returned from the Communist sector of Berlin, the colonel reported his conversation with the Russian to Army Intelligence. And after he reached the United States, he gave the full story to FBI agents.

The FBI immediately laid plans to see if the Soviets would try to get in touch with the colonel on any of the dates the Russian had mentioned in Berlin.

On October 15, agents stationed themselves near 86th Street and Madison Avenue. They saw two members of the Soviet representation to the Military Staff Committee of the United Nations walking around the area as though looking for someone.

"This fits the pattern of Soviet espionage, all right," an agent said. "They're looking for the colonel."

The next meeting date listed was October 25. With Mr. Hoover's approval, the New York espionage squad was to make a bold gamble: a special agent would be sent to the meeting place.

An agent was chosen who looked very much like the colonel. He was five-feet-eleven and weighed about 178 pounds. His brown hair was receding from his forehead. He had hazel eyes, ruddy cheeks, and a full face with a rounded chin. But he was ten years younger than the colonel and he didn't have the colonel's mustache.

A professional make-up artist was called in and shown photographs of the colonel. He touched up the agent's hair and face to make him look older. Then he fashioned a mustache from spirit gum and crêpe hair—placing each hair in place to make the mustache look natural.

When he was finished, the make-up man stepped back and said: "Well, what do you think?"

An agent exclaimed, "The colonel's own mother couldn't tell the difference!"

Off duty, the colonel liked to wear loose-fitting tweed jackets. So the agent got a loose tweed jacket. He was briefed on the colonel's family background and the assignment he had held in Berlin.

On October 25, the special agent arrived at 86th Street and Madison Avenue at about 4:05 P.M. As he stood on the northeast corner, other agents saw he was being watched by two Russians from the United Nations. But neither made any move to contact him.

Three weeks later the agent wore the same disguise and went to the same corner, where he stood waiting. This time a man walked up to him and mumbled something in a low voice.

"Pardon me," the agent said. "What was that?"

"Seems to me that I have met you at Spechstrasse," the man said. "Colonel, what is the number of your house there?"

"Oh, yes," the agent said. "I have lived there at Spechstrasse 19."

The man held out his hand. "My name is Schultz," he said, and suggested they go for a ride.

"If you don't mind," the agent said, "I'd rather walk in Central Park." And so the two men set out for the park.

Agents watching this little scene recognized the Russian immediately. He was Maksim Martynov, a member of the Soviet representation to the U.N. Military Staff Committee.

As they walked toward the park, the "colonel" asked if he would meet the Russian whom he had met in East Berlin. "Schultz" said no and indicated he had taken on this mission for his friend. Then the "colonel" showed the Russian his identification card.

They reached the park and walked along the reservoir. "Schultz" began asking questions about Leavenworth. The "colonel" rambled on with information that was accurate but not classified. The Russian insisted he must have specific facts about the Army post.

"Colonel," he said, "are you willing to help me?"

"It will be hard to do," the "colonel" said, "but it might be possible."

Before they parted, the Russian reached into his overcoat pocket and pulled out a roll of bills which he pressed into the "colonel's" hand. The agent stuffed the money into his pocket without counting it. Later he found it was $250 in ten-dollar bills.

Their next meeting was on January 15, 1955, on the same corner of Madison Avenue. They agreed to go to a nearby hotel bar before having dinner. As they walked toward the hotel, the "colonel" said: "I've got the information you want. It is right here in my briefcase."

They took a table in a dimly lit corner of the bar. "Schultz" cautioned his companion to speak in whispers.

"I've got what you want," the "colonel" said. "Do you have any paper on which to make notes?"

"No," the Russian said.

"Then you'll just have to remember what I have to say to you."

The Russian was nervous. As the "colonel" talked, it became more and more obvious that the Russian wished to get his hands on the briefcase and get out of the bar. "I don't like this place," he whispered.

At this point the "colonel" placed the briefcase on the table in front of him. FBI agents moved in on the table. The Russian protested he was merely having a friendly drink. When asked to produce his identification, he showed his United Nations credentials which listed his name—Maksim Martynov.

**Maksim Martynov, waiting, checks his watch.**

**FBI agent parades before Martynov.**

Martynov could not be arrested because he had the status of a diplomat. But the State Department stepped in and he was forced to leave the United States on February 26, 1955.

During the many years that FBI agents have been on guard against Soviet espionage, they also have kept watch on the leaders of the Communist Party in the United States. At one time the Party's membership reached 80,000 (1944). But the number of members didn't worry the FBI as much as the influence the Communists might have in government, unions, schools, business, and politics.

Martynov speaks code words of recognition to FBI agent.

A confident Martynov shakes hands with the FBI agent disguised as a retired army officer.

U. S. Communist Leader William Z. Foster, who died in Moscow in 1961, once said that the strength of the Communists could not be measured by numbers but "it has to be measured largely by the general mass influence of the Party and its programs." And in this case the FBI agreed with him.

The American people received one of their worst shocks when a fat man in rumpled clothes went before the House Committee on Un-American Activities in 1948 and confessed that he had been a spy for the Soviet Union. His name was Whittaker Chambers and he had been a senior editor for *Time* magazine.

Chambers admitted he once had been a member of the Communist Party for thirteen years. He said he received stolen documents from the Department of State and turned them over to Colonel Boris Bykov, a Soviet agent. As a member of Washington's secret Communist underground of the 1930s he named Alger Hiss, a trusted and brilliant young diplomat who had worked in the inner councils of the government. Hiss then appeared before the House Committee and denied the charges.

On August 17, 1948, the House Committee arranged for Hiss to confront Chambers in New York. At this confrontation, Hiss identified Chambers as a George Crosley whom he had known for a short period in Washington. And he challenged Chambers to repeat his Communist charges outside the Congressional hearing where he could be sued for libel.

Ten days later, Chambers repeated his charges before a nation-wide radio audience. Hiss sued him for $75,000, charging slander and libel.

Chambers then produced excerpts from State Department documents which he said were typed by Mrs. Hiss and given to him by Alger. He also produced four small pieces of paper, in the handwriting of Hiss, which he said were notes made from State Department documents by Alger Hiss. The accused man admitted that these four were in his handwriting; but he denied having ever given State Department material to Chambers or any other unauthorized person.

Chambers led investigators to his Maryland farm where he gave them microfilm which he had hidden in a pumpkin. The film contained photographs of more State Department documents.

The FBI had 263 agents working on the Chambers-Hiss case at one time or another seeking the truth of the charges and denials. The most important items of evidence they found were the documents in Chambers' hands which had been written on a Woodstock typewriter. Hiss had owned a Woodstock; and the agents tracked down papers which had been typed on that machine while it was in the Hiss household in the 1930s. Examination of these papers by the FBI Laboratory established that they and the documents brought to light by Chambers had been prepared on the same typewriter.

There was other evidence, too, linking Chambers with Hiss—enough to convince a jury that Hiss was lying when he denied turning over the papers to Chambers. He was convicted of perjury and sentenced to five years in prison.

Then came shock after shock as the FBI uncovered evidence that the Communists had stolen atomic secrets.

# 12. Trailing the Atom Bomb Spies

Soviet Russia's theft of atomic secrets from the United States during World War II has been called "the crime of the century." And this crime began on December 3, 1943, when the British ship *Andes* slipped into the harbor at Norfolk, Virginia.

The Atlantic crossing had been dangerous for the *Andes* with Nazi U-boats roaming the ocean like wolf packs looking for prey. It was only natural that the passengers and the ship's crew should laugh and joke now that the danger was behind them.

Among those at the ship's rail were a small number of British scientists. Their arrival was so secret that no word of it would reach the newspapers. Only the President of the United States and a few other people knew they were here to work with American and Canadian scientists in an effort to build the world's first atomic bomb.

No one knew for certain that such a bomb could be made. But President Roosevelt had given the go-ahead signal to try it. And that's why Klaus Fuchs, a brilliant young physicist, was at the rail getting his first glimpse of the United States. His eyes were big behind the thick-lensed glasses he wore.

As Fuchs waited for the signal to go ashore, an older scientist walked up and stood beside him.

"There it is, Klaus," he said. "And I'm bloody glad to be here."

"I'm glad, too," Fuchs said. "I have never been in the United States before."

"Oh, you will find old friends . . ."

Fuchs shook his head.

"No," he said, "I have only a sister in Cambridge, Massachusetts."

It was true that Klaus Fuchs knew no one well in America except his sister and her husband. But he said nothing of the fact that somewhere out there a man was waiting . . . waiting to receive the information Fuchs would pass on to him.

Fuchs did not know the name of this Stranger. But the Stranger would know him and he would recognize the Stranger. They would meet. He would give the Stranger the information. And whatever he gave him would reach Russia. That was how it had been in England . . . and that's how it would be in the United States because Fuchs was a Communist.

There was no delay in getting ashore at Norfolk and no questions asked. The United States Army—which was directing the secret atomic project—accepted the word of the British that all the scientists aboard the *Andes* could be trusted.

And soon the scientists were on their way to New York to see the sparkle of lights for the first time in many months. It was an exciting contrast to their own country where the lights had been blacked out each night because of German bombers.

A few weeks after Klaus Fuchs arrived in New York, he left his room at the Barbizon Plaza Hotel one wintry day. He took a subway train to New York's Lower East Side. Then he walked along the street with a white tennis ball clutched in his hand.

Fuchs had not gone far when he saw the Stranger. He knew him because the man was carrying gloves and a book with a green binding. He was a chunky, middle-aged man with a round face.

The Stranger came toward Fuchs and said: "It's good to see you. Come with me." Fuchs stuffed the tennis ball into his overcoat pocket. It had served its purpose.

They stepped into a taxi and the driver took them to a restaurant on Third Avenue. When they were seated, the Stranger said, "I am Raymond." Never would he tell Fuchs that his real name was Harry Gold.

Fuchs told Raymond about the super-secret project hidden behind the name Manhattan Engineer District. He told him of the crash effort to solve the many problems involved in making an atomic bomb. He promised to get facts, figures, and formulas and to deliver them as soon as possible. They made plans to meet again and then they parted.

For five years their meetings remained a secret. . . .

In early September, 1949, Director Hoover sat in his office in Washington, D. C., and studied a top-secret report which chilled him with shock and anger. There was no doubt about it. Somehow, foreign agents had stolen the secrets of how to build and detonate an atomic bomb. The FBI was not responsible for atomic security in the early 1940's; the job had been turned over to the FBI by Congress in the Atomic Energy Act of 1946.

Hoover issued orders to his agents which said in effect: "The secret of the atomic bomb has been stolen. Find the thieves."

Agents hurried to the Los Alamos atomic plant near Santa Fe, New Mexico, and to other plants. They searched records and files and talked to hundreds of people who had worked on different parts of the project.

It soon became clear that the key figure in the theft probably was not an American. The chances were that he was a physicist and had been a member of a foreign mission. This narrowed the field of suspects sharply.

As the hunt was underway, President Truman gravely announced that the government had evidence "that within recent weeks an atomic explosion occurred in the U. S. S. R." There was little doubt about it: the Soviets had saved many months and even years of research through the theft of atomic secrets.

Bit by bit, the evidence pointed to Klaus Fuchs. But Fuchs was now the respected chief of the Theoretical Physics Division in Great Britain's nuclear energy center at Harwell, England. He seemed above suspicion. He had no known interest in politics or much of anything outside his work. Women talked of him as a "sweet and shy" man.

But then parts of the puzzle snapped into place. An agent came across the name Klaus Fuchs while searching through Gestapo records seized by American intelligence officers during the war. The file was headed: "Klaus Fuchs, student of philosophy, December 29, 1911, Russelsheim, RSHA-IVA2, Gestapo Field Office, Kiel."

Perhaps there were many men named Klaus Fuchs in Germany—but this one had the same birth date and birthplace as the Klaus Fuchs who had worked as a physicist at the Los Alamos atomic center. It was hardly likely that two persons with the same name would be born on the same day in the same city.

The initials RSHA were those of the

Central Office of Security Police. The Roman numeral IV was a department within the central office. A2 was the number of the file in which the Germans placed the names of people believed to be Communists.

This fact alone was not proof that Fuchs was a Communist. The Gestapo could have had the names of many innocent people in that file merely because they were opposed to the Nazis. But this bit of information fitted too neatly with another discovery.

In 1946, the Canadians had broken up a Soviet spy ring in which a well-known scientist was a key figure. Canadian police had picked up an address book in which appeared the entry: "Klaus Fuchs, 84 George Lane, University of Edinburgh, Scotland." The information uncovered in this case had been given to the FBI.

At that time, the name meant nothing to the FBI because the Bureau had not taken over the job of guarding atomic security. But now the entry in the address book was important because it was another finger pointing to Klaus Fuchs.

Hoover passed this information about Fuchs to the British Intelligence Service (MI5) and their agents began shadowing him while checking into his background. Within a month they were certain that Fuchs was a spy for the Communists.

Three months after the FBI began looking for the key man in the puzzle, British Security Officer William J. Skardon called on Fuchs at his flat. He told the physicist he was suspected of passing secrets to the Russians.

"I don't think so!" Fuchs exclaimed.

"That's no answer," Skardon said.

"I do not understand," Fuchs said. "Perhaps you will tell me what the evidence is. I have not done any such thing."

**Klaus Fuchs.**

From time to time, Skardon returned to question Fuchs only to get the same denials. But one day Fuchs sent word he wished to see Skardon.

Again the officer knocked on his door. "You asked to see me and here I am," he said.

"Yes," Fuchs said, "it is rather up to me now."

It was clear to Skardon that Fuchs was in a highly nervous state. He began talking of his hatred of the Nazis and his sympathy for the Communist cause. He talked of his fear for the safety of his father who still lived in the Red zone in Germany. He talked of everything but espionage.

Skardon listened and then quietly asked Fuchs if he didn't want to clear his conscience by telling the truth of what had happened.

"I will never be persuaded by you to talk," Fuchs said.

The two men had lunch together. And then it was that Fuchs broke down. He confessed he had given nuclear secrets to the Russians for eight years. They had not made the first advance. He had gone to them and offered his help in 1941. Then he began turning over information to a Soviet contact.

When he was chosen to go to the United States, he told his contact about it. The Russian agent told him that on a certain day he should go to a certain street on New York's Lower East Side carrying a tennis ball in his hand. He would see a man carrying gloves and a book with a green binding. This man would be his contact in the United States.

Fuchs confessed he had met the Stranger a good many times while he was working at Los Alamos. He was a man about forty or forty-five years old, chunky of build, about five-feet-ten, and had a round face. He wasn't a physicist but he knew chemistry well—and perhaps he was a chemist. He called himself "Raymond." That was about all that Fuchs knew of the Stranger.

Fuchs' arrest was announced by the British on February 3, 1950. Hoover sent a cable to Sir Percy Sillitoe, chief of MI5: "Congratulations on a job well done. Your coöperation in this case is much appreciated. Regards."

A Senate-House committee would say of Fuchs: "It is hardly an exaggeration to say that Fuchs alone has influenced the safety of more people and accomplished greater damage than any other spy not only in the history of the United States but in the history of nations."

Klaus Fuchs was brought to trial in the London court known as Old Bailey. His attorney argued that when Fuchs became a British citizen in 1942, "He was a known Communist, and he had never pretended he was anything else . . . Anybody who had read anything about Marxist theory must know that a man who is a Communist, whether in Germany or Timbuctoo, will react in exactly the same way. When he gets information, he will automatically and unhappily put his allegiance to the Communist idea first."

Lord Chief Justice Goddard said to Fuchs: "You have betrayed the hospitality and protection given to you with the grossest treachery. . . ."

Fuchs was sentenced to fourteen years in prison.

For the FBI the question now was: "Who was the Stranger to whom Fuchs had given the secrets?" Fuchs said they had met at least ten times, in New York, Santa Fe, and Cambridge, Massachusetts. There wasn't much to go on except that the man knew chemistry and might have been a chemist.

FBI agents called on Fuchs' sister, Mrs. Kristel Heineman, and her husband in Cambridge. Could they remember a heavy-set, middle-aged man who came to see Fuchs when he was visiting them?

The Heinemans did recall that in January, 1945, a heavy-set man came to the house and asked for Klaus, who was coming to spend his vacation with them. The man had returned later and Klaus seemed to know him. They had talked together for quite a while. Mrs. Heineman remembered that the visitor was fond of children. He had told her son he was going to send him a chemistry set.

The Heinemans' description of the Stranger tallied with that given by Fuchs. And here again was the mention of chemistry.

Agents began the search for a chemist who would fit the description of the Stranger. Very likely he had worked in the New York area during the mid-1940s. But this could be only a guess. Even if the search were limited to New York City alone, the task was enormous. In 1945, the city had issued 75,000 licensing permits to chemical firms.

But the search had to be made. One by one the names were dropped from the list of chemists until the name of Harry Gold remained. He was working in the heart station of the Philadelphia General Hospital.

Agents called at Gold's home at 6823 Kindred Street in Philadelphia. He was shown a picture of Klaus Fuchs and asked if he knew the man.

"This is a very unusual picture," Gold said. "He is that English spy!" He added that he recognized Fuchs from the pictures he had seen in the newspapers but they had never met.

Did he know Mr. and Mrs. Heineman in Cambridge? Had he ever visited Santa Fe, New Mexico? Gold said he didn't know the Heinemans and as a matter of fact he had never been in New England or traveled west of the Mississippi river.

Agents questioned Gold several times. At last they asked if they might search his home. "I've told you everything I know," he said. "I've got nothing to hide. If it will help, go ahead and search the place."

Gold said his bedroom would be a good place to start since that was where he kept most of his papers, books, journals, and letters. He seated himself in a chair and settled down to watch the search.

Foot by foot, the agents began going over the room. One of them pulled a bookcase away from the wall and noticed by the dust that it had not been

**Harry Gold.**

moved for a long time. Then he saw a yellow folder which had slipped behind the bookcase. It was a map of Santa Fe, New Mexico.

The agent spread the map on a table and said: "You said you had never been west of the Mississippi? Or have you?"

Gold stared at the map for a long minute of silence. For some reason he made no effort to lie out of it. He said: "I . . . I am the man to whom Klaus Fuchs gave his information."

Once he started talking, Gold poured out the story of how he began spying for the Soviets in 1936, turning over industrial secrets which he thought would help the Soviet Union grow stronger.

He had become mired deeper and deeper into this pit until it was too late to turn back. ". . . the realization that I was turning over information to (Russia) . . . was so frightening that the only thing I could do was to shove it away as far back in my mind as I could and simply not think on the matter at all . . ."

He said each time he got information from Fuchs, he turned it over to a Soviet agent he knew only as "John"—later identified as Anatoli A. Yakovlev, Russian Vice Consul in New York.

Bit by bit, the FBI pieced together the shameful story. It went like this:

Gold continued his meetings with Fuchs through 1944 and into the summer of 1945. In May of 1945 he met Yakovlev at a small bar and restaurant in New York to discuss his next meeting with Fuchs in Santa Fe.

Yakovlev told Gold that after seeing Fuchs, he must go to Albuquerque to the home of an American sergeant. The sergeant was working at the Los Alamos atomic plant as a machinist and he had some very important information.

Gold protested it was dangerous to see both men on the same trip because it might expose Fuchs. But Yakovlev said: "You go! That's an order!"

The Russian wrote the name "Greenglass" on a sheet of onionskin paper along with an address, 209 North High Street. Below the name he wrote: "Recognition signal. I am from Julius." Then he handed Gold a piece of cardboard cut from a Jell-O box. Gold was to give the cardboard to Greenglass as a part of his identification, and also give him an envelope containing $500.

Gold arrived in Santa Fe on June 2, 1945. As he wandered around the city, he stopped at a newsstand and picked up a Chamber of Commerce map—a yellow folder which said "Santa Fe, The Capital City." He tucked it into his pocket. It was the same map which the FBI agent would find almost five years later behind the bookcase.

Gold went to an agreed meeting place. Soon Klaus Fuchs drove up in an old car and Gold climbed into the seat beside him. They drove to a lonely spot where Fuchs handed Gold a packet of papers containing atomic bomb secrets. He also told him something known only to a few men: The first atomic bomb was to be tested at Alamogordo, New Mexico, the next month!

After meeting Fuchs, Gold rode a bus to Albuquerque. He arrived on a Saturday night and found that the Greenglasses were not at home. He spent the night in a boarding house and next morning went to the address given to him by Yakovlev.

Sergeant and Mrs. Greenglass had just finished breakfast when Gold knocked at the door.

The sergeant opened it.

"Are you Mr. Greenglass?" Gold asked.

"Yes. Won't you come in?"

Gold stepped into the living room and said: "I come from Julius."

"Oh," Greenglass said, "you arrived sooner than I expected." He picked up his wife's purse and took out a piece of cardboard. Gold handed him his part of the Jell-O box and when Greenglass put them together they matched perfectly.

"Have you any information for me?" Gold asked.

"I have some," Greenglass said, "but I will have to write it up. If you come back later, I'll give it to you." He introduced Gold to his wife, Ruth.

Gold returned in the afternoon. Greenglass gave him sketches of a triggering device being used in the atomic experiments. He also listed the names of people he thought might be recruited for espionage in the Los Alamos plant. Gold left the $500 with Greenglass and carried the information from Fuchs and Greenglass to New York where he turned it over to Yakovlev.

When the FBI followed the trail to Greenglass, he denied that he knew Gold or that he had given him any information. But finally he confessed that what Gold said was true.

Greenglass told agents that in August of 1944 the Army sent him to work at Los Alamos. Three months later his wife, Ruth, arrived from New York to spend a few days with him. It was the second anniversary of their marriage.

One day his wife told him of a talk she had had in New York with Ethel and Julius Rosenberg. Ethel was David Greenglass's sister and Julius was his idol. He had always thought more of Julius than any man he knew.

Ruth said Julius had told her that he and Ethel had stopped their Communist Party activities and even had quit reading the *Daily Worker,* the Party newspaper.

David could hardly believe this to be true because Julius and Ethel had always been loyal Party workers. They had persuaded him to join the Young Communist League when he was fourteen. He had only joined because he admired Julius so much.

"But why?" David asked.

Ruth said: "Julius said at last he's doing what he always wanted to do—giving information to the Soviet Union." She added that Julius knew David was working at the atomic bomb center. And Julius wanted David to give him any information he could that would be useful to Russia. Julius argued that the Soviet government deserved to have this information—and it would be better if the atomic secrets were known by all nations.

"I can't do that," David said. But the next day he agreed. He gave Ruth a description of the Los Alamos layout and also the names of scientists who were working there. Ruth Greenglass carried this information to Julius when she returned to New York.

When David came to New York on leave two months later, he made a number of sketches of a lens mold for Julius —at his request—and gave him the names of people who might be willing to work for the Soviets.

Julius told Ruth Greenglass that she could go to Albuquerque to live with David and he would pay her expenses. The money would be a gift, he said, from the Russians.

Later that night, the question came

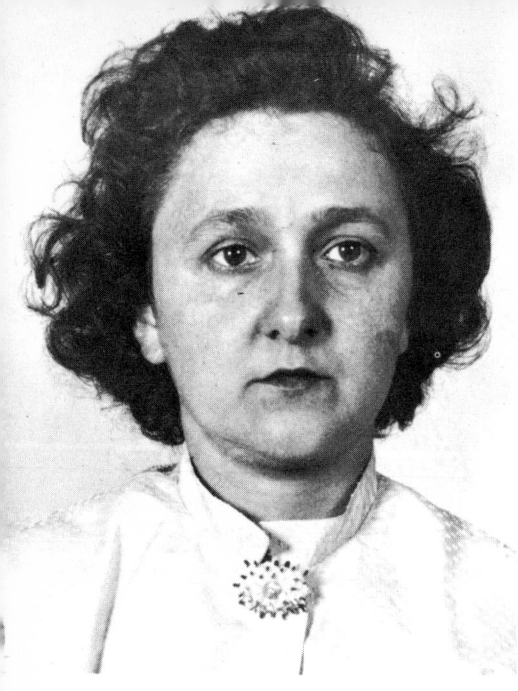

Ethel Rosenberg.

Julius Rosenberg.

up of how Greenglass would be able to recognize a messenger sent by Julius.

"Well," Julius said, "I'll give you something so that you will be able to identify the person who does come."

Julius went into the kitchen with Ruth and his wife and cut two pieces of cardboard from the side of a Jell-O box so that the end of one piece fitted into the end of the other. He handed one half to Ruth Greenglass who put it in her purse.

Ruth went to live with David at Albuquerque. But they came back to New York on furlough after the atomic bombs were dropped on Hiroshima and Nagasaki and Japan had surrendered. This time Greenglass gave Julius a cross-section sketch of the Nagasaki-type bomb, drawn from his own knowledge and what he had heard from scientists and others at Los Alamos. He also gave his brother-in-law and sister a handwritten report on the work at Los Alamos. That night, they sat in the Rosenbergs' living room while Ethel typed the information David had written.

When the British announced the arrest of Klaus Fuchs, Julius Rosenberg came to the Greenglass's apartment. He was excited and asked David to go with him for a walk in Hamilton Fish Park.

"You remember the man who came to see you in Albuquerque?" Julius asked.

Greenglass said he did.

"Fuchs was also one of his contacts," Julius said. He explained he was afraid that Gold would be caught and there was danger Gold might tell of his visit to Greenglass.

Julius urged Greenglass to leave the country at once. He gave him traveling instructions and a total of $5,000 in cash. He pleaded, argued and threatened. But Greenglass refused to run.

This was the story of espionage and betrayal pieced together by the FBI in countless hours of searching for the truth. The evidence gathered by agents left no doubt with a jury. The Rosenbergs were found guilty of espionage against their own country. They were sentenced to death and Greenglass was sentenced to fifteen years in prison.

Looking down at Julius and Ethel Rosenberg in the courtroom, Federal Judge Irving Robert Kaufman said: "I consider your crime worse than murder. . . ."

# 13. The Death of a Boy

Crime often reaches from the back alleys into the most unlikely places . . . as it did one day in 1953 in Kansas City, Missouri.

It was about 10:55 on the morning of September 28 when a plump, middle-aged woman rang the doorbell at the French Institute of Notre Dame de Scion, an exclusive school operated by Catholic Sisters for small children.

Sister Morand hurried to see who it was calling at this hour when the children were busy in their classes. She saw that the woman at the door was highly nervous and she asked her to step inside.

"I'm the aunt of Bobby Greenlease, Jr.," the woman said. Then she explained that Bobby's mother had been rushed to St. Mary's Hospital after suffering a heart attack. Mrs. Greenlease wished to see her son and the family had sent her to bring Bobby to the hospital at once.

Sister Morand said: "Of course. I understand." She was terribly sorry to hear of Mrs. Greenlease's illness. She asked the woman to wait in the chapel while she went upstairs to get six-year-old Bobby from the classroom.

Sister Morand told Bobby his aunt was waiting to take him home but she said nothing of his mother's heart attack. When she brought him downstairs, the boy gave no sign that the woman was a stranger to him. Perhaps he was too excited and confused.

The visitor whispered to Sister Morand: "I've been praying that Bobby's mother will recover. I'm not a Catholic and I don't know whether God heard my prayers."

Sister Morand assured her she was certain the prayers were heard. She watched with sympathy as the woman put her arm around the boy's shoulder and led him from the school to a taxi standing at the entrance. The cab driver had brought her to the school and waited while she went inside.

"Just let us out at the Katz parking lot at Fortieth and Main," the woman said, patting Bobby's hand.

The driver let his passengers out at the parking lot in downtown Kansas City. The woman led the boy quickly to a Plymouth station wagon. "Okay, let's get going," she said to the man waiting behind the wheel.

The driver was a ruddy-faced man with an old scar on his forehead. He swung the station wagon into the traffic and headed south toward Highway 169.

It was about this time that a Sister at the Institute called the Greenlease home to ask about Mrs. Greenlease and to say that Bobby was on his way to the hospital with his aunt. She was horrified to learn that Mrs. Greenlease was well and had not been taken to the hospital. She had not asked for her son to be taken away from the school and the woman who had walked away with Bobby was not his aunt.

Terrified by this call, Mrs. Greenlease called her husband, a wealthy automobile dealer. He rushed home to find out what had happened and to comfort his wife. The police were notified and they in turn called the FBI to report the kidnaping.

As the Plymouth station wagon drove south from Kansas City, Bobby Greenlease, Jr., sat between his captors in the front seat.

The man behind the wheel was thirty-four-year-old Carl Austin Hall, the son of a well-known and respected lawyer. The woman was Bonnie Brown Heady, forty-one. Hall had drunk and squandered away a sizeable fortune left to him by his mother and father. When the money was gone, he had turned to robbing taxi drivers in Kansas City. He was caught and sentenced to prison for five years. But he was paroled after serving only sixteen months.

Hall had not been out of prison very long when he met Bonnie Heady. While the two of them were drinking heavily one night in her home at St. Joseph, Missouri, they planned the kidnaping of Bobby Greenlease, Jr.

The first part of their plan worked so well that they saw no reason why they should not go all the way with it. They drove southward for a time and then Hall turned the station wagon onto a side road. After driving about two miles he swung the car into a narrow lane and switched off the engine.

Bonnie Heady got out and walked away from the car into a field. She didn't want to see what was happening behind her where Carl Hall had his fingers around the neck of the struggling boy. He held him with one hand while he reached into his pocket for a pistol.

"I had the gun in my coat pocket," he would tell FBI agents later. "I pulled it out and I shot once trying to hit him in the heart. I don't know whether I hit him or not for he was still alive . . . I shot him through the head on the second shot.

"I took him out of the car, laid him on the ground, and put him in a plastic

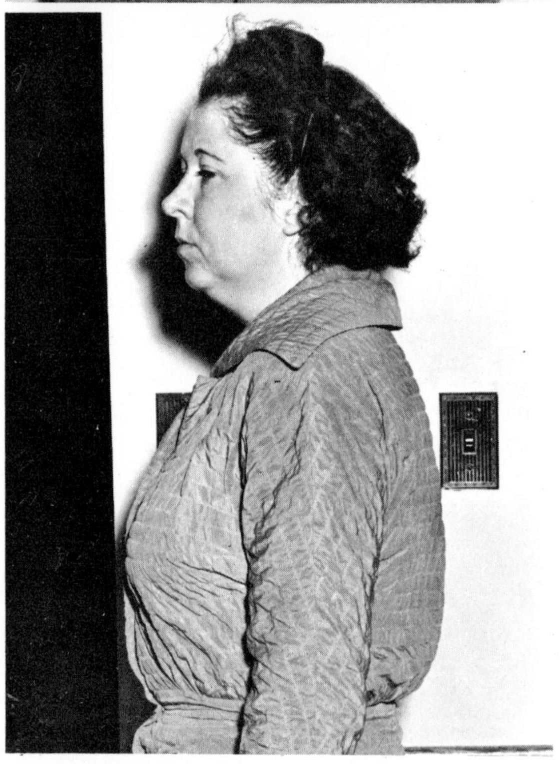

**Carl Austin Hall.**

**Bonnie Heady.**

bag. I remember a lot of blood there. This farm where the killing occurred is about two miles south and two miles west of the state line and in the state of Kansas."

After Hall had wrapped the body in the bag, Bonnie Heady came back and helped him put it into the back of the station wagon. Then they drove to her home in St. Joseph and parked the car in the garage. There was no one to see them as they took the body from the car. They placed it in a shallow grave which already had been dug beside the house.

Hall got a sack of quicklime from the garage and poured it over the body. Then he covered it with earth. The next morning Hall brought several chrysanthemums and planted them in the loose soil of the grave.

The Greenleases didn't have to wait long to hear from the kidnapers. Within a few hours Greenlease received a letter saying:

> Your boy been kidnapped get $600,000 in $20's—$10's—Fed. Res. notes from all twelve districts we realize it takes few days to get that amount. Boy will be in good hands—when you have money ready put ad in K. C. Star. M —will meet you in Chicago next Sunday—*Signed* Mr. G.
>
> Do not call police or try to use chemicals on bills or take numbers. Do not try to use any radio to catch us or boy dies. If you try to trap us your wife your other child and yourself will be killed you will be watched all of the time. You will be told later how to contact us with money. When you get this note let us know by driving up and down main St. between 39 & 29 for 20 minutes with white rag on car aeriel.
>
> If do exactly as we say an try no tricks, your boy will be back safe withen 24 hrs—afer we check money.
>
> Deliver money in army duefel bag. Be ready to deliver at once on contact.
>
> —M
>
> $400,000 in 20's
> $200,000 in 10's

This was the first of a series of messages to the Greenleases giving them hope that their son was alive and would be returned to them after payment of the ransom money. The Kansas City police and the FBI remained in close touch with the Greenlease family, but they did nothing that would interfere with a contact being made between the Greenleases and the kidnapers. This was the family's wishes.

Soon the Greenleases received a telephone call from the mysterious "M" and he was told the money was ready for delivery. They also received letters and calls giving instructions on how and when to deliver the money. But in each case something went wrong and the money was not delivered.

During one call taken by a friend of the Greenleases, Mrs. Greenlease demanded to speak to "M."

MRS. G. "M, this is Mrs. Greenlease."

VOICE. "Speaking."

MRS. G. "We have the money but we must know our boy is alive and well. Can you give me that? Can you give me anything that will make me know that?"

VOICE. ". . . A reasonable request, but to be frank with you, the boy has been just about to drive us crazy. We couldn't risk taking him to a phone."

MRS. G. "Well, I can imagine that. Would you do this? Would you ask him two questions? Give me the answer of two questions?"

VOICE. "Speaking."

MRS. G. ". . . If I had the answer to these two questions, I would know my boy is alive."

VOICE. "All right."

MRS. G. "Ask him what is the name of our driver in Europe this summer."

VOICE. "All right."

MRS. G. "And the second question: What did you build with your monkey blocks in your playroom the last night you were home? . . . If I can get those answers from you, I'll know you have him and he is alive, which is the thing you know that I want."

VOICE. "We have the boy. He is alive. Believe me. He's been driving us nuts."

MRS. G. "Well, I can imagine that. He's such an active youngster."

VOICE. "He's been driving us nuts."

MRS. G. "Could you get those answers?"

VOICE. "All right."

But Hall never called with any answers to these questions. He sent messages telling the Greenleases where to find notes he had left under rocks marked by crayons or taped to the bottoms of mailboxes. These notes were like clues in a grisly game of "Treasure Hunt." They gave directions to the hiding places of other notes. But they became so confusing that no one knew where to deliver the money. After each failure the family would wait to hear from "M" again.

One night a go-between drove into the country with the $600,000 stuffed into a duffel bag. He tossed the bag—weighing eighty-five pounds—to the side of a lonely country lane and left it for the kidnapers. But once again "M" called to say he had searched for the bag and couldn't find it in the darkness. The money was recovered during the early morning hours by friends of the Greenleases.

"M" made his fourteenth telephone call to the Greenleases' home at 8:28 P.M. on October 4, 1953. The call was taken by Robert Ledterman, a close friend of the Greenleases. It went like this:

LEDTERMAN. "Greenlease residence. Ledterman speaking."

VOICE. "How are you?"

LEDTERMAN. "Fine. How are you tonight?"

VOICE. "A little late."

LEDTERMAN. "You said eight o'clock. Are we all set?"

VOICE. "We're all set. We have a perfect plan. It couldn't be any . . ."

LEDTERMAN. "How's that now? Give me that again?"

VOICE. "There could not be any mistake. This is a perfect plan. It will have to be a little later. I am sorry, too, but we want to make sure there's no mix-up this time."

LEDTERMAN. "Yes. Let's get things over—say, by the way, M, did the boy answer any of those questions?"

VOICE. "No . . . I couldn't . . . we didn't get anything from him."

LEDTERMAN. "Couldn't get anything from him?"

VOICE. "He wouldn't talk . . . I'll tell you this much. You will get him in Pittsburgh, Kansas."

LEDTERMAN. "You're not bunking me in that, are you?"

VOICE. "That's the gospel truth . . ."

That night Ledterman and a friend, Norbert S. O'Neill, loaded the bag of money into a car. It was about midnight

**Photograph of the duffel bag in which the Greenlease ransom money was placed. After removing the $600,000, Carl Hall discarded the duffel bag in the large trash can shown behind it in a St. Louis, Missouri, alley on October 5, 1953.**

when they dropped the bag beside a bridge near the junction of Highways 40 and 10E near Kansas City.

A short time later "M" called to say he had found the money but he hadn't had time to count it. Ledterman gave him assurances that the bag held the $600,000 just as "M" had demanded.

VOICE. "Well, I'm sure of that. You can tell his mother that she will see him as we promised within twenty-four hours . . . We will certainly be very glad to send him back."

Never did Carl Hall and Bonnie Heady let the Greenleases know that their son was lying dead beneath the chrysanthemums outside the house in St. Joseph.

Once the money was in their hands, they went to an apartment on Arsenal Street in St. Louis and promptly got drunk. During the night, Carl Hall slipped away from Bonnie Heady while she was asleep. He left only $2,000 of the ransom money in her purse.

When Hall was drinking, he liked to talk. And he talked too much to a taxi driver who tipped St. Louis police that he could give them "something hot." The tip led police to Hall and Bonnie Heady who were arrested on the night of October 6—eight days after the murder of Bobby Greenlease, Jr.

Hall confessed to police and FBI agents. The body was found in its shallow grave. Agents recovered thirty-eight-caliber shell casings which the FBI Laboratory found had been fired by the pistol Hall was carrying at the time of his arrest. There was a bullet under the floor mat of the station wagon owned by Bonnie Heady. It had the same markings made by Hall's gun. Bloodstains were found at the Heady house and on one of the woman's nylon blouses.

Bonnie Heady admitted she helped Hall write the ransom notes and that she lured Bobby from the school in Kansas City. But she tried to place all the blame for the killing on Hall.

Hall and Heady pleaded guilty to the kidnap-murder, and a jury recommended death sentences. Judge Albert L. Reeves sentenced them to die in the gas chamber of the Jefferson City State Penitentiary. He said: "I think the verdict fits the evidence. It is the most cold-blooded, brutal murder I have ever tried."

And the $600,000? Only $298,040 was recovered. What happened to the rest of the money remains a mystery which the FBI is still trying to solve.

Among all the records on crime since World War II, one of the most disturbing has been the number of young people in trouble with the law. In 1962 the arrests of youths under eighteen were nine per cent greater than in 1961. Over a period of twelve years (1950–62) the under-eighteen arrests by police had jumped 133 per cent.

Questioned about youth crime figures by a committee of Congress, Director Hoover said in his opinion much of the blame fell on parents. Among the causes he cited were broken homes, lack of discipline, and too little love and affection. But he insisted that young hoodlums arrested for serious crimes should not be treated merely as "juvenile delinquents" but as "juvenile criminals" whom society has the right to hold responsible for their acts.

Bank robberies increased, with the "lone bandit" appearing more often than in earlier years. But sometimes an entire family helped stage robberies as one did in Wisconsin. A gang made up of a mother, her twenty-four-year-old son, fourteen-year-old daughter, and two others outside the family were involved in this crime in which a bank

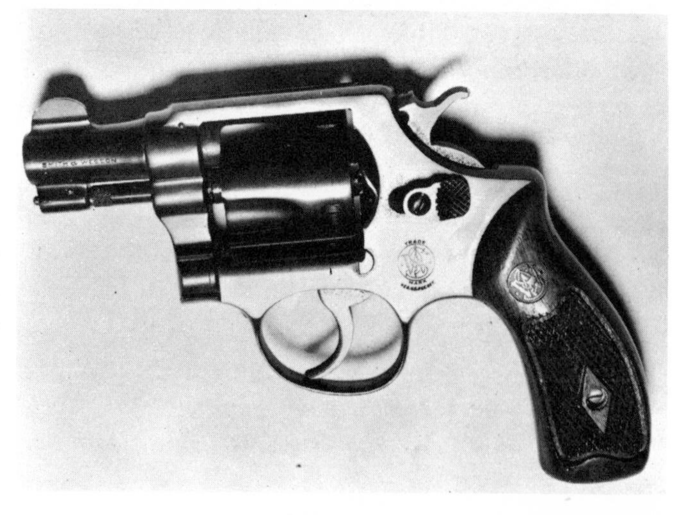

**.38 caliber Smith & Wesson revolver taken from Carl Austin Hall at time of his arrest and which he used to kill the victim, according to his confession to Bureau agents.**

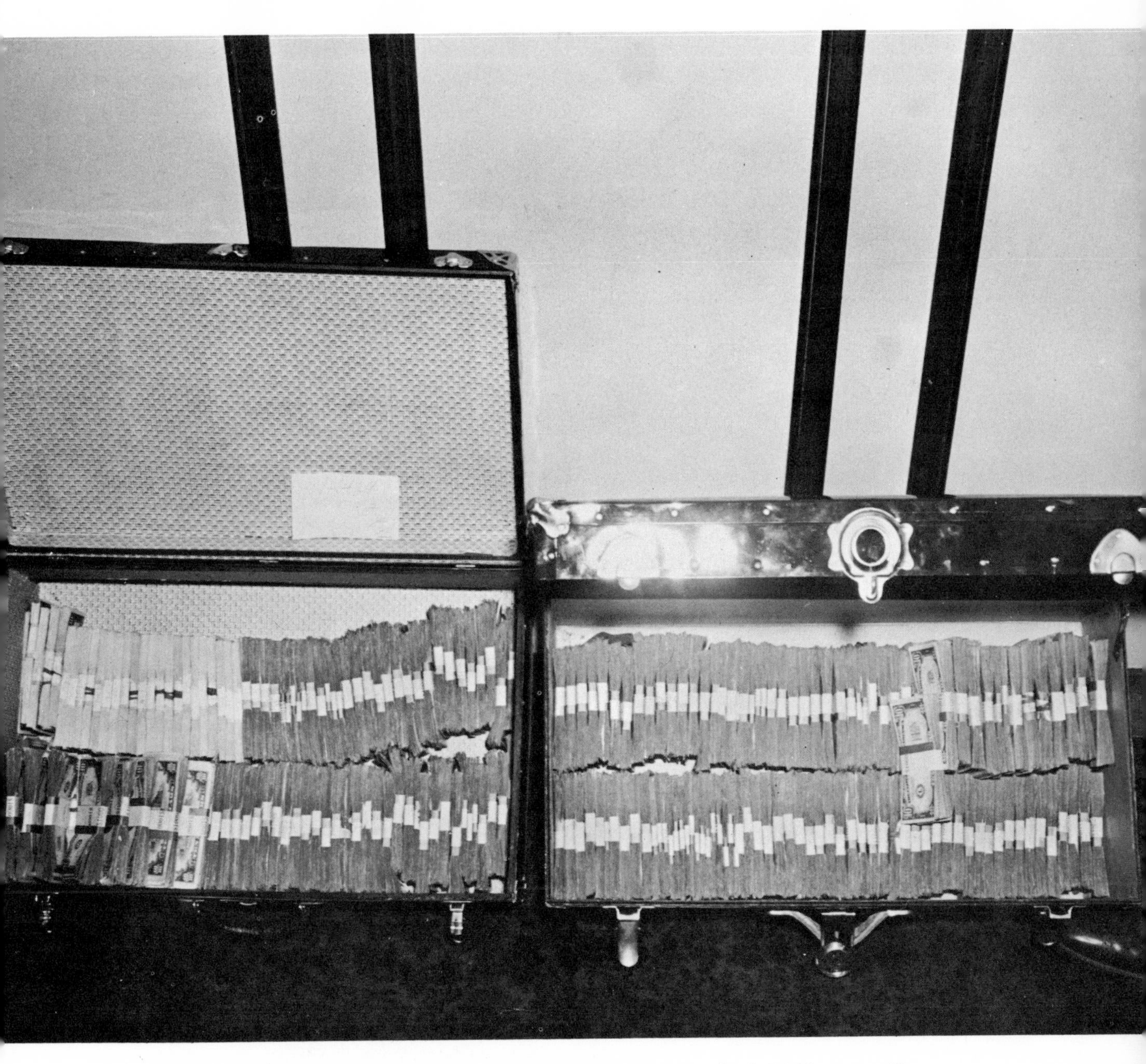

Two metal suitcases containing approximately $293,000 which Hall reportedly had in his possession at the time of his arrest.

was looted of $11,533.93.

The daughter carried a gun during the robbery. The next school day she handed her teacher a note signed by her mother which said: "Please excuse Marguerite, she was sick with a cold." Her brother said proudly to agents: "I don't know what she would have done if somebody had started shooting, but I think she would have done all right."

Gangsters such as John Dillinger, "Baby Face" Nelson and "Old Creepy" Karpis no longer roamed the land terrorizing people as they did in the 1930s. But the boom years following the war were rich ones for nation-wide gambling syndicates, big-city racketeers, and hoodlums hiding their operations behind business and union fronts. Hoover estimates that crime is costing the nation $22,000,000,000 each year.

In 1961, Congress passed a series of laws giving the FBI greater powers to move against organized crime and racketeering. And today a new drive is underway against the underworld. The FBI's fight against crime is still a battle that has no ending.

# 14. A Christmas Gift of Murder

Mrs. Daisie King could not know that death was only a little more than one hundred minutes away when she closed the lid on her battered old suitcase and strapped it shut late in the afternoon of November 1, 1955, at her home in Denver, Colorado.

She walked into the living room where her twenty-three-year-old son, Jack, sat with his wife, Gloria, and their young son, Allen.

"Jack," she said, "you can put the suitcase in the car now. I've finished with the packing."

"Sure, Mother," the young man said as Mrs. King opened the door and walked from the house with her daughter-in-law and grandson. Jack was a big fellow, standing more than six feet tall and weighing one hundred ninety pounds. He was Mrs. King's son by her second husband and his last name was Graham. His father had died before he was five and then his mother had married a wealthy rancher named King.

Jack Graham went to the living room, picked up the heavy suitcase with ease, and took it to his car. But instead of packing it directly in the trunk, he loosened the straps and opened the lid. He lifted out a toilet kit and a few items of clothing. In their place he put a special package which his wife had earlier been told was a Christmas gift.

A faint ticking noise came from the package. But when Graham closed the lid, the ticking could not be heard. He then locked the trunk and climbed in on the driver's side of the car.

Mrs. King had been looking forward to this trip. She was flying to Alaska to spend the Christmas holidays with her daughter.

The Grahams drove with Mrs. King to the airport and Jack helped carry her suitcase, a small traveling case, and a brief case to the United Air Lines ticket counter. The luggage was thirty-seven pounds overweight and the ticket agent said the extra charge would be $27.

"My goodness!" Mrs. King exclaimed. "I had no idea the bags would be that heavy."

The agent suggested that she still had time to open the big suitcase and take out anything she wished because her plane was a few minutes late. She could save money by mailing some of her clothing to Alaska.

Mrs. King said to her son: "Do you think I'll need all this?"

"Yes, Mother," he said, "I'm sure you will need it."

While she was busy at the ticket counter paying the extra charge, Jack Graham began feeding quarters into a machine which sold $6,250 worth of life insurance for each quarter dropped into the slot. He filled out two policies which would pay him a total of $75,000 in case of his mother's death. He bought two others for $6,250 each, writing in the names of an aunt in Missouri and his half-sister in Alaska. In his fumbling haste, he ruined one policy for $18,750 and another for $43,750.

Mrs. King signed three of the policies but for some reason didn't sign one for $37,500. Perhaps it was because the time had come for her to board Flight 629 which was on its way to Portland, Oregon.

Other passengers bought a great deal of insurance that evening, too—far more than usual. Eighteen men and women insured their lives for a total of $752,200 and this did not include any other life insurance they might have had.

The Grahams walked with Mrs. King to the loading gate. She kissed them good-by and hurried to get aboard. Jack Graham stood watching the plane, waiting nervously for it to start moving. Perhaps it was the ticking noise in his mother's suitcase that was pounding in his ears—making him more nervous with each passing second.

But at last the plane door was slammed shut behind a late passenger and the DC-6B moved out onto the runway. At 6:52 P.M. the big ship raced down the runway and lifted into the dusk. It carried thirty-nine passengers and a crew of five.

The Grahams went into the airport coffee shop for a snack. But Jack Graham, his face white, bolted from the table and went into a restroom to vomit. His wife thought he looked better when he returned to the table.

Flight 629 hurtled through the sky with the early lights of Denver fading behind. The plane was eleven minutes from the airport and flying at about 5,700 feet when a beet farmer stepped out of his barn below and saw the plane's dark outline against the sky.

He watched the wing lights blinking and then in one paralyzing second he saw the plane disappear in a ball of fire. The thunder of an explosion reached his ears. Flaming gasoline spilled down in streamers from the sky. A flare burst into brilliant light and slowly burned itself out. And then it was all over.

The farmer was a witness to one of

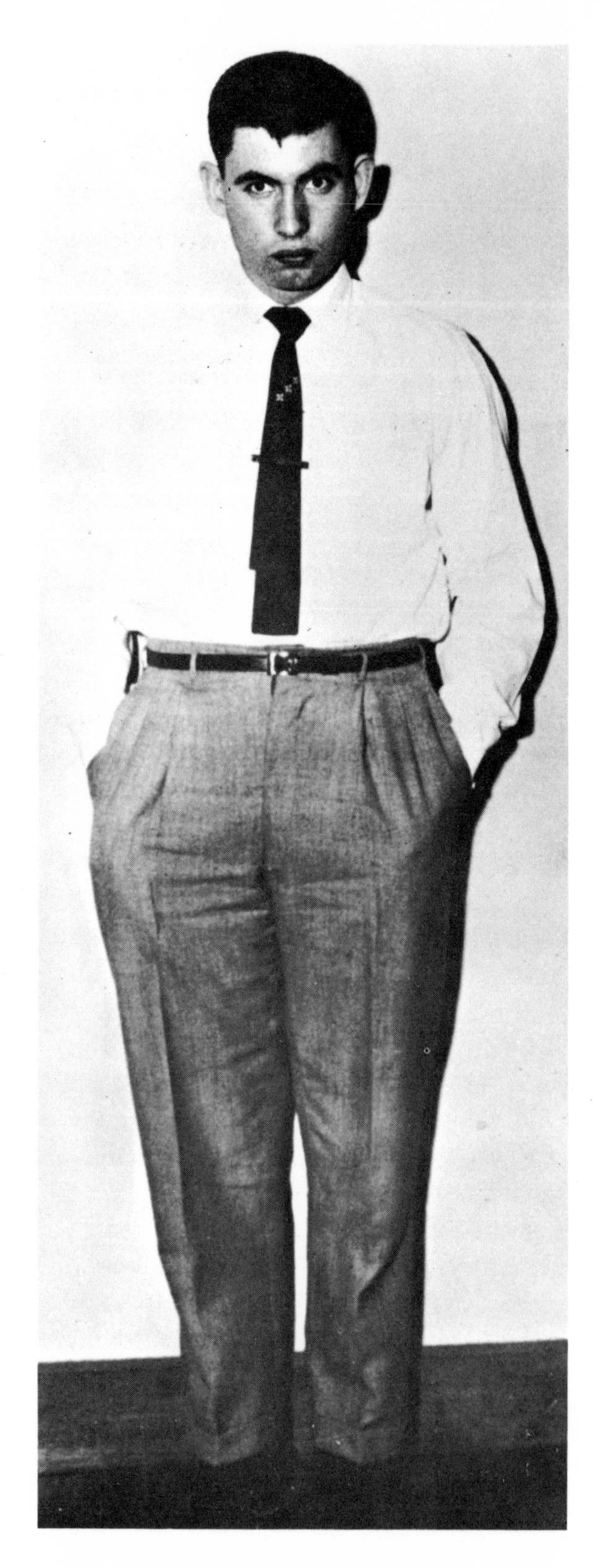

**Jack Gilbert Graham.**

the most horrible mass murders in American history, although only one man knew that night what had happened. Jack Graham knew, when he heard the rumor of an airplane crash before he left the airport with his wife and child.

News of the crash reached Roy Moore, assistant special agent in charge of the FBI's Denver office, as he sat at home watching television. The United Air Lines (UAL) was immediately told that the FBI was prepared to help in any way possible. Then Moore furnished his headquarters in Washington, D. C., all available details of the crash.

Later that night when it was certain there were no survivors, the UAL's flight surgeon asked for FBI help in identifying the bodies. The Civil Aeronautics Board asked that an FBI Laboratory expert be sent to the crash scene to help examine the wreckage and look for the cause of the crash. Agents from the FBI Disaster Squad—organized in 1940 for just such emergencies as this—arrived in Denver the next day.

The wreckage of Flight 629 was scattered over two square miles along with the broken bodies and the luggage. A tail section of the plane was all in one piece as though it had been sliced from the other part by a huge knife. It lay a mile and a half from the point where the nose of the ship and the engines had plowed into the ground.

The experts asked themselves: Was the crash caused by mechanical failure? Was it the result of human error? Or was it sabotage? The idea that someone had deliberately wrecked the plane was the least likely of all.

The investigation of the Colorado plane crash will always be a striking example of the progress made by the FBI in scientific law enforcement from the day in 1924 when Hoover took command of the Bureau.

The bodies were carried from the scene to the National Guard Armory at Greeley, Colorado. Nine were quickly identified by friends and relatives or by personal effects. FBI agents took the fingerprints of thirty-five others and identified twenty-one of them from prints on file in the FBI Identification Division at Headquarters. Most of these twenty-one persons had been fingerprinted during service with the armed forces or while working in defense plants and government offices. One man had filed his fingerprints with the FBI so there would be a permanent record of his identification in case of a disaster such as this one.

The FBI Laboratory expert joined in the search for the cause of the crash with others from the United Air Lines, Douglas Aircraft Company, and Civil Aeronautics Board.

The crash area was first divided into huge squares which were numbered. Crews of men began picking up pieces of the plane and the scattered luggage. Each piece was carefully marked to show the exact spot on which it was found in the numbered squares. Then the parts were taken to a warehouse in Denver. A model of the plane's fuselage was built of wood and wire netting. And investigators began the slow task of fitting the pieces of metal into the places where they had been before the plane was ripped apart.

The shell of the big ship became almost complete—except in one place near the right side of the tail. There was no metal found to fit into a jagged hole where the Number 4 cargo pit had been.

Part of wreckage of DC-6B airliner which crashed near Longmont, Colorado, November 1, 1955. These are parts of the inner skin from the door of the #4 Cargo Compartment.

Around the hole, the edges of the metal had been bent outward by a force which appeared to have come from inside the plane. Pieces of metal were found which were shiny on one side and burned on the other. Bits of metal had been hurled through the soles and heels of shoes, and the brass fitting from a suitcase had been driven into a stainless steel container.

It was clear to the investigators that no ordinary plane crash could throw bits of metal about as though they were shot from a gun. Samples of the metal which had been burned were sent to the FBI Laboratory for tests.

All the evidence pointed to a violent explosion in cargo pit Number 4. Since there were no gasoline lines in this part of the plane, there could have been no gasoline fumes in the pit. The blast had to be from a package of explosive material shipped illegally—or from a bomb planted by a saboteur.

As soon as this fact was clear, the CAB asked the FBI to make an investigation of possible sabotage. Some one hundred agents in twenty cities began digging into the backgrounds of the plane's passengers, looking for an enemy with a motive for murder. They also checked on the boxes and parcels shipped on the plane on the chance that someone had mailed a box of explosives.

The first faint suspicion of Jack Graham came when agents were unable to find Mrs. Daisie King's luggage. It did seem strange that her bags were the only ones in the cargo pit to be totally destroyed. And then agents found her handbag which she had carried with her to her seat. Inside the bag was a four-year-old newspaper clipping which had a story about Jack Graham: he was wanted by police for forgery.

As other possible suspects were cleared, the FBI began to center attention on Graham. Agents found that he had been a restless, brooding boy with a vile temper and a mother who pampered him. He had gone to work in 1951 for a Denver manufacturer as a payroll clerk. He stole some of the company's checks, forged the name of a company official and cashed them for $4,200. He paid $2,000 for a flashy convertible car and took off on a spree that led through five states. It ended in a hail of bullets at a police roadblock in Texas.

Mrs. Daisie King got her son out of this scrape. And Jack seemed to be going straight for a time. He married a Denver girl, Gloria Elson, and they had two children. His mother invested $35,000 in a drive-in restaurant and turned it over to Jack to manage, since her third husband had died.

Agents heard reports that Jack had tried to collect insurance twice on "accidents" that looked suspicious to the insurance people. Once it was a damaged truck and the next was a gas explosion in the restaurant.

Agents questioned Jack Graham for the first time on November 10, nine days after the crash. They asked about Mrs. King's luggage and what she had in it.

"I don't know what she put in her luggage," Graham said. "Mother liked to pack things herself and she never let anyone help her. I do know she took some shotgun shells and rifle ammunition with her. She was planning on doing some hunting in Alaska."

The next day they talked to Gloria Graham. She said that Mrs. King had packed her own bags. But she added that her husband had taken a gift-wrapped package to the basement that afternoon before they left for the airport. She thought it was a Christmas gift Jack had bought for his mother—a set of tools for making costume jewelry. Mrs. King liked to make jewelry from sea shells.

The story of the gift-wrapped package was something new. Graham had said nothing about a package or a set of tools for his mother. Agents made discreet inquiries among Graham's neighbors, asking if they knew anything about a Christmas gift Jack had bought for his mother.

One neighbor said: "I heard Jack say he had searched the town to find the kind of kit he wanted. Jack said he had gift-wrapped it and placed it in his mother's luggage as a surprise for her when she reached Alaska."

Another neighbor reported that Jack and his mother often fought "like cats and dogs" and one remembered him saying, "I'd do anything for money."

Only two stores in Denver sold the type of tools used in cutting sea shells. Agents found that neither of them had sold a single tool kit during the month of October. They decided to ask Graham to explain about the gift.

Jack Graham and his wife came to the FBI office in Denver on Sunday afternoon, November 13. They were asked if they could identify pieces of luggage that might have been from Mrs. King's bags. Gloria stayed for a few minutes and returned home to the children while agents continued to question Graham.

Late that afternoon, Special Agent Roy Moore called the FBI Laboratory to ask about the results of the test made on the pieces of burned metal.

"There is positive evidence of a dynamite explosion," he was told. The metal showed traces of chemical compounds which are left by exploding dynamite.

"Thanks," Moore said. "That's a big help."

More certain than ever that he was on the right track, he went back to the room where Graham was sitting.

"I want you to know you have certain rights," Moore said to Graham. "The door is open. You can walk out any time you wish. There is a telephone. You can call your wife or an attorney if you wish. You don't have to tell us anything—and if you do it can be used against you in a court of law. There will be no threats and no promises made while we talk to you.

"Jack," he said, "we have gone over what you told us. You blew up that plane to kill your mother, didn't you?"

"No, I didn't," Graham said angrily.

"Then do you mind if we search your home?"

"No, I don't mind," the youth said. He signed a waiver giving agents permission to search his home without waiting to get a search warrant.

Agents hurried to the Graham home. After a time, one of them called Moore and said: "Mrs. Graham says Jack told her not to tell about the Christmas present. She signed a statement."

Later, they found the shotgun shells and ammunition which Jack said his mother had taken in her luggage. This information was passed on to Moore.

"What about that Christmas present for your mother?" Graham was asked.

He explained that he had bought an X-Acto tool set from "some guy" he didn't know. He had paid $10 for it and two of his friends had been present when he bought it. He had bound the box with Scotch tape, wrapped it as a gift, and slipped it into his mother's bag as a surprise. He had left the roll of tape in the glove compartment of his car.

There was no Scotch tape in the car. But agents did find in one of his shirt pockets a roll of wire, the kind used on electric dynamite caps. They also found the $37,500 insurance policy signed by Mrs. King. It was hidden in a cedar chest in Graham's bedroom.

Graham's two friends were asked if they had seen him buy a set of tools from a stranger. Both said no.

Agents pointed out to Graham the growing number of conflicting statements in his story. He was told about the FBI Laboratory report that a dynamite explosion had caused the plane crash.

By this time the hand of the clock on the wall had slipped past midnight. Jack Graham said, "Can I have a glass of water?"

An agent filled a glass and Graham took a long, gulping drink. He set the glass on the table and said: "Okay, where do you want me to start?"

"Wherever you want to."

"Well, it all started about six months ago. Mother was raising the devil because the drive-in wasn't making any money . . ."

With no trace of regret, Jack Graham recalled how he planned his mother's murder. The fact that forty-three other persons also died that night did not seem to matter to him.

He said he worked for ten days in an electric shop to learn more about electricity. Then he bought twenty-five sticks of dynamite which he taped together and hooked up to a six-volt battery, a timer, and two primer caps. This was the "Christmas package" he had slipped into his mother's suitcase.

Graham's confession was taken down by a stenographer and he signed it. Then a doctor was called to the FBI office to give him a thorough examination. The agents were taking no chances on Graham claiming that he had been beaten and forced into signing the confession. They also wanted a doctor's opinion that he was of sound mind.

When these things were done, Graham was arrested for sabotage. Later he was turned over to Colorado authorities to be tried for murder.

The story Graham told was checked out by agents. They found the places where he had bought the dynamite and the timer. He was identified by those who had made the sales. A jury convicted him of first degree murder and recommended the death penalty. On January 11, 1957, Graham was executed in the gas chamber at the Colorado State Penitentiary.

In the Colorado plane crash, the FBI used the scientific methods and means of investigation developed over a period of thirty years. Among these were: (1) the identification of victims by their fingerprints; (2) the Laboratory tests of the metal showing a dynamite explosion had taken place aboard the plane; (3) the patient gathering of evidence by men trained for such work; (4) the coöperation with local police, other agencies, and townspeople; (5) getting a signed confession without threats or force of any kind; (6) the clear presentation of facts to the persons responsible for prosecuting criminal offenders; (7) and the teamwork between the men in the field and the men in the FBI Headquarters in Washington, D. C.

Many years ago, the Bureau chiefs in Washington knew little about what the men were doing out in the field. But that loose and disorganized kind of operation ended when Hoover took over.

Today Hoover's office keeps a tight, around-the-clock check on the agents and the cases on which they are working. At any time he chooses, the Director can pick up his telephone and find out where an agent is at any hour of the working day, the case on which he is working, and the progress being made.

The secret of the FBI's disciplined operation—if it can be called a secret—lies in its leadership. While Hoover is "Mr. FBI"—the man who did the building—he has trained an inner circle of top-flight executives who came up through the ranks of special agents.

Hoover once said of these men: "You can't buy the kind of energy and devotion they have given to the FBI."

The Director's right-hand man is Associate Director Clyde Tolson of Laredo, Missouri, who joined the FBI in 1928. At that time he planned to stay only a few months and then open his own law office in Cedar Rapids, Iowa. But, as many others do, he decided to make the FBI his life's work.

Next to Tolson are two Assistants to

**Executives of the FBI.**

MR. HOOVER
*Director*

MR. MOHR
*Assistant to the Director*

MR. TOLSON
*Associate Director*

MR. BELMONT
*Assistant to the Director*

**MR. ROSEN**
*Assistant Director*

**MR. TROTTER**
*Assistant Director*

**MR. DE LOACH**
*Assistant Director*

**MR. CALLAHAN**
*Assistant Director*

**MR. CONRAD**
*Assistant Director*

**MR. EVANS**
*Assistant Director*

**MR. TAVEL**
*Assistant Director*

**MR. SULLIVAN**
*Assistant Director*

**MR. CASPER**
*Assistant Director*

**MR. GALE**
*Assistant Director*

the Director, John P. Mohr and Alan H. Belmont. Under the direction of these three are ten Assistant Directors, each in charge of a Division. The Divisions are: Identification, Training, Administrative, Files and Communications, Domestic Intelligence, General Investigative, Laboratory, Crime Records, Special Investigative, and Inspection.

These men meet each Monday and Wednesday at 10:30 A.M.—or daily in special cases—for the "FBI Executives Conference." Tolson presides and each man is expected to say what he thinks about any problem that arises whether it is in his own Division or not. The conference is no place for "yes men."

The executives don't always agree on a course of action. When this happens, the different recommendations are passed on to Hoover and he makes a final decision. Once the decision is reached, the men walk out as a team, knowing where they are going and what must be done.

It is a system that has helped to make the FBI one of the most famous crime-fighting organizations in the world.

# 15. Fingerprints and the Scientist

Among the hundreds of millions of people in the world there are tens of thousands who look alike. Total strangers sometimes look as though they might be brothers. Parents can't always tell one twin from another and neighbors exclaim: "They're as much alike as two peas in a pod."

But there is one readily identifiable mark which every man carries with him from birth to death that is different from all others. It is his mark—and his alone. There is no other like it. And this mark is his fingerprints.

Many years ago Mark Twain wrote the make-believe story of a young Missouri lawyer who amused himself by having people put their fingerprints on pieces of glass. Then he would file the prints away along with the names and date on which the prints were taken. Over the years he collected scores of prints for his file.

It was such a strange hobby that people around town didn't think the lawyer, David Wilson, was very bright. They began to call him "Pudd'nhead."

The town changed its mind about Pudd'nhead after he was called on to defend twins accused of murder. It looked as though the twins were certain of being convicted until Pudd'nhead brought into court the fingerprints he had kept on glass through the years.

He told the jury:

> Every human being carries with him from his cradle to his grave certain physical marks which do not change their character, and by which he can always be identified—and that without shade of doubt or question. These marks are his signature . . . and this autograph cannot be counterfeited, nor can he disguise it or hide it away, nor can it become illegible by wear and mutations of time . . . This autograph consists of the delicate lines or corrugations with which Nature marks the insides of the hands and the soles of the feet. If you will look at the balls of your fingers . . . you will observe these dainty curving lines lie close together, like those that indicate the borders of oceans in maps, and that they form various clearly-defined patterns, such as arches, circles, long curves, whorls, etc., and that these patterns differ on the different fingers . . . One twin's patterns are never the same as his fellow-twin's patterns . . .

He went on to prove by his fingerprint file that the twins were innocent, the murderer was someone who had not been suspected, and the tragedy could be traced to a nursemaid who had deliberately switched two babies in their cribs.

Mark Twain wrote his story before the time that fingerprints began to be widely used as a means of identifying criminals. But it is no stranger than the tales that can be found today in the records of the FBI Identification Division.

In these records are cases in which crimes have been solved, families have been re-united, missing persons located, and men and women saved from prison—sometimes even from death—by means of fingerprints.

The finding of only a part of a fingerprint in 1928 saved four men from going to prison and perhaps from being hanged in Colorado. It happened in this way:

On the morning of May 23, 1928, four men walked into the First National Bank of Lamar, Colorado, and drew pistols. "Put up your hands! This is a stick-up!" the leader shouted.

The frightened bank employees and customers threw up their hands and watched in amazement while the bandits quickly gathered up $219,000 in cash and bonds.

For the first few seconds, Bank President A. N. Parrish was too startled to do anything but sit at his desk watching the robbers loot his bank. And then anger flooded over him. He reached into his desk drawer and grabbed a pistol. He fired at one of the bandits and blood spurted from the man's face.

The wounded bandit shot Parrish dead. The banker's son rushed to his father's side and he was shot down, too. The gang forced E. A. Lungren, bank teller, and Everett A. Kessinger, assistant cashier, into their waiting car. They raced from town with their two hostages and the fortune in money and bonds. A short distance away, they shoved Lungren out of the car.

Sheriff Lloyd E. Alderman gave chase in his car, armed only with a pistol. But his weapon was no match for the rifles of the bandits. The heavy bullets from their guns knocked out the Sheriff's car and the bandits escaped.

That night a man called at the home of Dr. W. W. Weininger at Dighton, Kansas, about 155 miles from the scene of the robbery. The man said: "Doc, you've got to come with me. My neighbor was driving a tractor and got himself smashed up. He's in bad shape. I walked here as fast as I could."

Dr. Weininger hurried from the house with the stranger and they drove away in the doctor's car.

A posse found the body of Kessinger, the assistant bank cashier, in an abandoned shack. He had been shot to death. Not far away they located Dr. Weininger's wrecked automobile. The doctor's body lay in a ravine nearby. He had been shot, apparently after he had treated the wound of the bandit shot by banker Parrish.

Officer R. S. Terwilliger came from the Garden City, Kansas, police department to check the doctor's car for fingerprints. It looked to him as though someone had taken a rag and gone over the car to wipe away any fingerprints. But he continued the search.

While going over the glass on the right rear door of the car, he found part of a fingerprint near the top of the glass. He took the glass out of the door and carried it to Garden City to develop a print.

Two months later, an enlarged photograph of the partial print was sent to the FBI on the chance that it could be identified by the Bureau files. But at that time the Bureau had 2,000,000 prints on file and they were classified only on a ten-finger system. A search for part of a single print was more than the Bureau could undertake.

Hoover heard of the problem and told the fingerprint experts: "It's a long shot, but I want you to memorize the pattern of that print. Impress it on your memory, and it may be you will come across the print some day. I know it's unlikely, but it's the only thing we can do."

Months later, four men were arrested and charged with the bank-robbery

**Preliminary fingerprint classification on incoming fingerprint cards being determined by Fingerprint Classifying Unit, Technical Section, FBI Identification Division, Washington, D.C.**

murders. Sixty persons said they were certain that the accused men were the bank robbers. But some officials felt there was doubt enough to delay their trial.

One day in 1929, more than a year after the robbery, the sheriff of Stockton, California, mailed to the FBI a set of fingerprints taken from a train robbery suspect who gave his name as William Harrison Holden.

The card was turned over to Fingerprint Expert Albert B. Ground. In a routine check, Ground discovered that the prints of Holden matched those of Jake Fleagle, who once had served time in Oklahoma for robbery. There was no doubt about it. William Harrison Holden's real name was Jake Fleagle.

He put Fleagle's card aside to continue with other work. But then he picked it up again and studied the prints. There was something about the print of the right index finger that kept nagging at his memory. Ground was like an expert in map-making who sees a bit of a map and then tries to remember where it fits into the whole.

Suddenly he thought of the partial print from the murder case in Colorado. He went to the files and got the old photograph. When he matched it with Fleagle's prints, he saw they were the same. It was Fleagle, alias Holden, who had left his fingerprint on the window of the doctor's car.

This information was telegraphed to police in California and Colorado. It was the clue which put officers on the trail of the four bank bandits. Fleagle was killed in a gun battle. His three pals were caught, tried, and hanged. And the four men who had been suspected of the crime were freed of the murder charges.

Men have known for centuries that fingerprints were different in their patterns. In ancient China men used a thumbprint in clay as their "signature." Fingerprints have been found on early Chinese and Japanese legal papers—and monarchs sometimes used fingerprints on wax as a royal seal.

The first widely-used method of identifying criminals was invented in the 1880s by Alphonse Bertillon of France. It was based on the idea that no two people could possibly look alike and at the same time have the same body measurements. Police took a criminal's head, arm, finger, leg and foot measurements and kept them on file with his photograph.

Many police officials clung to this idea of Bertillon's until one day in 1903 when a Negro named Will West was brought to the Federal Penitentiary at Leavenworth, Kansas. He was first taken to the record clerk's office to be photographed and measured.

The record clerk looked at the prisoner and said: "I've seen you before. Don't we already have your measurements?"

Will West shook his head. "No, sir," he said. "I've never been here before."

The clerk took West's measurements with the Bertillon instruments, going from his head to his feet. But when he went to file them he saw there already was a card on file under the name "William West." The measurements on the card were almost exactly the same in every detail as those he had just taken. The face on the photograph was the image of Will West.

"Why did you tell me you had never been here before?" the clerk demanded.

Initial processing of fingerprint cards to record date of receipt, assign priority and indicate type of reply, Recording Section, FBI Identification Division, Washington, D.C.

"Here's your picture."

Will West looked at the photograph. "That looks like me, all right," he said. "But I've never been in this prison before."

And then the clerk realized that Will West was telling the truth. The look-alike William West at that moment was in his cell in the Leavenworth prison, serving a life sentence for murder. The Bertillon system had failed.

The Will West-William West case gave support to those who had been urging that the old system be replaced by the fingerprint system of identification. England's Scotland Yard already had dropped the Bertillon system in favor of fingerprints after Sir E. R. Henry had worked out a simple way to classify them.

The International Association of Chiefs of Police (IACP) was the first to campaign for a central fingerprint file which would serve all police agencies. The IACP got support from the American Bar Association and in 1921 the Department of Justice agreed to set up an Identification Division in the Bureau of Investigation.

Masses of fingerprint files and Bertillon records were shipped into Washington from police and prison officials. But the Bureau had no funds with which to set up a Division. For eight months the files lay piled in boxes and packing cases. The country's criminal identification system was bogged down.

This was part of the confusion Hoover found when he became FBI Director. He talked to members of Congress and with backing from others persuaded them to give the Bureau $56,320 to bring order out of this chaos. Within sixty days the service was restored.

At first the fingerprint file contained only some 800,000 sets of prints, all of them of persons who had been involved in crime. Later the FBI set up a Civil Identification section whose files were kept separate from the criminal files. People were encouraged to place their fingerprints in the Civil file for permanent identification. By early 1963, the Bureau had the fingerprints of 14,700,000 persons in the criminal files and prints of 62,400,000 persons in the Civil file.

The criminal files have helped police across the nation solve uncounted crimes. They also have saved many men from going to prison.

In one case, John "The Bug" Stoppelli was arrested in San Francisco on a charge of peddling narcotics. It wasn't the first time that "The Bug," a notorious hoodlum, had been in trouble with the law. A fingerprint examiner who claimed to be an "expert" testified that a partial finger impression on an envelope containing narcotics was made by the left ring finger of Stoppelli.

Stoppelli protested it was not his fingerprint, but he was sent to prison. Only his lawyer believed his story, and the lawyer continued to protest until the FBI was asked to compare the fingerprint on the envelope with Stoppelli's file. The check showed that the print had not been made by the convicted man.

A Federal official said: "No matter how low a man may be, he has civil rights. So we sent the FBI's report back to the U. S. Attorney in San Francisco." As a result, President Truman commuted Stoppelli's sentence.

In other cases, the civil fingerprint file has proved to be valuable in identifying

Training class for fingerprint technicians, Technical Section, FBI Identification Division, Washington, D.C.

victims in airplane crashes, laboratory explosions, ship disasters, and other accidents. It has helped bring together members of families who became lost from each other in childhood.

Hoover once received a letter from a man in Wisconsin asking the FBI's help in locating a brother he had not seen in more than thirty years. The brother's name was found in the civil files because his fingerprints had been taken when he applied for a wartime job. The card gave his address as Milford, Connecticut.

This information was sent to the man in Wisconsin. Soon a letter came back: "I tried a long-distance telephone call at the address given. My brother answered the phone, the first time I had heard his voice for thirty-three years. . . . . you did more for me in one day than I have been able to do in years of inquiry and of following up leads that always led nowhere."

The Identification Division is never closed. The work goes on around the clock in relays, speeding information to police throughout the country—a service that is given without charge. Often the FBI coöperates with other nations in fighting international crime. Fingerprint data is exchanged with seventy-eight non-Communist nations as well as the Canal Zone, Guam, Puerto Rico, and the Virgin Islands.

During a recent twelve-month period, fingerprints helped the FBI and police in locating 17,568 men and women wanted by authorities in different parts of the country. Never a day passes that they do not help trap a murderer, a bank robber, an escaped convict, or someone else who is running from the law.

In December, 1961, a man stumbled into a town in the Florida Keys, looking gaunt and hungry. He told a story of escaping from Cuba in a rowboat and braving the seas, sharks, and storms to get away from the Red regime of Fidel Castro. He said he took off his clothes and made them into a sail which he hoisted on his rowboat. Then he was driven by the winds to the Keys. He said he was Mario Levi, a native of Italy.

As usual in such cases, he was first taken into custody by the United States Immigration and Naturalization Service officers; and his fingerprints were sent to the FBI's Identification Division.

Mario Levi's story was a hoax. His fingerprints showed that he was Mate Ivanov who had escaped from a New York mental institution three weeks earlier. Police had been looking for him as a suspect in the brutal murders of five persons at Mineola, New York.

Along with the fingerprint division, the FBI's Laboratory in Washington, D. C., has proved over the years to be a place where crimes often are solved by experts hundreds of miles from the scene of a murder, a robbery, or some other crime.

Such a case came to the Laboratory in 1936 when it was only four years old and the Bureau was feeling its way along in the new field of using scientists as crime detectives. Experts bending over their test tubes and microscopes were able to point the finger of guilt at a killer in faraway Alaska.

There were no witnesses to the murder in a remote place called Old Buckland Village. The reason was that the killer crept toward the home of his victim under cover of a March blizzard. He slipped to the sheltered side of a cabin and peered through a window at the man he was going to kill.

Taking fingerprints for personal identification purposes, FBI Identification Division, Washington, D.C.

The victim was John Nilima, a weather-beaten prospector and trader. His home was a trading center where the Eskimos brought their furs to sell for money or to exchange for food, clothes, traps, and guns. When not trading with the Eskimos, John usually could be found in the hills searching for the gold which he dreamed would make him rich.

The killer at the window raised his rifle and sent a bullet crashing through Nilima's head. The trader never knew what hit him. The crack of the rifle was lost in the howling of the winds. The killer then slipped into the cabin, robbed the cash box, and then disappeared into the storm. The snow and wind covered his tracks.

Nilima's body was found on March 17th. Word of the murder was sent to the United States Marshal at Nome, Alaska, and he came to Old Buckland Village to investigate. The only clue was the rifle bullet which had torn through Nilima's head and lodged in a log. The marshal dug it out and dropped it into his pocket.

The marshal rounded up two suspects. The first man was an ex-convict who had once threatened to kill Nilima during an argument over gold prospecting. The marshal noticed stains on the man's socks that looked like dried blood.

"Is that blood on your socks?" he asked.

"Yes," the ex-convict said. "I shot a reindeer and some of the blood dropped on my socks while I was dragging it home."

"Can you show me the carcass?"

"Sure," the man said. "Let's go right now."

There was no carcass where he said it would be. "Maybe the wolves dragged it off a ways," the suspect said. But there was no trace of the animal to be found.

The marshal looked at the ex-convict's thirty-caliber rifle and saw that it had not been cleaned since it was last fired. "I'd better take that rifle with me," the marshal said.

His second suspect was a young Eskimo. He had been spending money freely at a nearby trading post and then had set out toward the northeast. He was caught on the trail and brought back for questioning. He carried a twenty-five-thirty-five-caliber rifle.

Both men claimed they were innocent and it began to look as though the marshal had no case against either of them since there were no witnesses. But then he recalled reading about a new crime laboratory in which the FBI would examine any evidence sent to them by police officers. He bundled up the suspects' rifles, the bloodstained socks, and the bullet found in the wall. He mailed them to the FBI Laboratory.

The Laboratory quickly determined that the blood on the socks was not human blood. A ballistics expert fired a shot from the ex-convict's rifle into a cotton-filled box. He took the bullet from the cotton and compared the markings on the bullet with those on the bullet which killed Nilima. They were not the same.

This test was made because each gun has tiny, rough spots in its barrel—no matter how smooth it may look to the naked eye. Each gun leaves its own pattern of lines and grooves on the bullets which hurtle through its barrel. Thus it is possible—in all but the most unusual cases—to match a bullet with the gun which fired it.

The expert then fired a shot from the

Eskimo's gun. It was placed under a microscope alongside the death bullet. The bullets were turned under the microscope until the agent saw that the tiny grooves made by the gun barrel were exactly the same on both bullets. There was no doubt left. The bullet which killed the trader in his cabin had been fired from the Eskimo's rifle.

These findings were sent to the marshal in Nome. The ex-convict was freed and the Eskimo confessed to the murder. He was sentenced to prison for twenty years.

Sometimes it may be a speck of dirt which gives agents the clue that a suspect was at the scene of a crime. The dirt from the sole of a shoe worn by a suspect is sent to the Laboratory along with a bit of dirt from the crime scene. These two pieces of dirt are placed in twin furnaces under intense heat. If both bits of dirt undergo certain changes at exactly the same times—and the changes are recorded automatically on a graph—then they contain exactly the same minerals. And they could have come from the same place.

The Laboratory experts are all special agents with the same training as the men who work in the field. They know the practical problems of the field agents and police, and what to look for in the evidence that is sent to them. Often they are able to lift a cloud from the lives of people suspected of a crime. They did this in a case in Luray, Virginia.

In February, 1950, a shot sounded in the home of Mr. and Mrs. Robert F. Parks in Luray. Mrs. Parks ran from the house to a neighbor's. She cried that her husband had been shot and she needed help. The police were called.

When Luray police walked into the Parks home, they found Parks dead. The body of the former Army captain was lying in a bedroom which opened off the dining room. An automatic pistol lay on the dining-room floor against the wall across from the bedroom door. The cartridge case was jammed in the gun.

When Mrs. Parks was able to talk, police officers questioned her about what had happened.

"I was in the kitchen when I heard the shot," she said. "I ran to the bedroom and Bob was standing there. He looked at me and said, 'Honey, the gun backfired.' And then he fell." She said she and her husband were alone in the house when the shot was fired.

Parks had been shot from the right side. The bullet had gone through his right arm, entered his chest, passed through his heart, and lodged on his left side. The direction from which the bullet came and the absence of powder burns on his arm ruled out the chance that Parks might have been holding the pistol when it fired.

The police learned that the Parkses quarreled violently at times. One person had heard Mrs. Parks call San Francisco and ask someone to send her a Luray-to-San Francisco bus ticket.

Even though there were no witnesses to the shooting, all the evidence seemed to point to Mrs. Parks. She was arrested and charged with murder.

The Luray police continued their search for more facts. An officer returned to the Parks' house to study the scene of the killing. As he stood in the doorway between the dining room and bedroom, he noticed a shiny place on the metal grille over the hot-air duct at his feet.

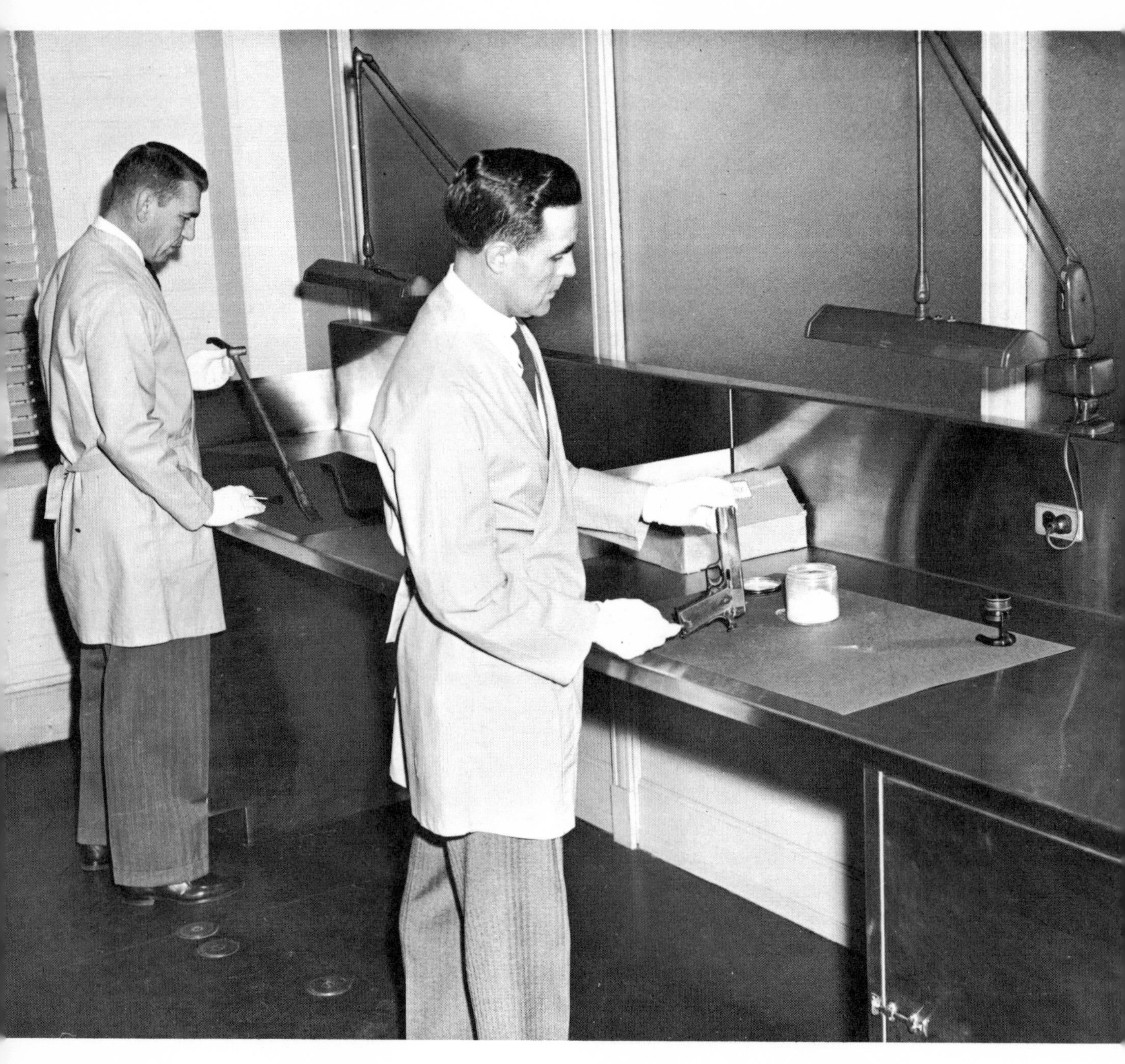

**Fingerprint technicians examining evidence for latent fingerprints by using dusting powder to show fingerprints, FBI Identification Division, Washington, D.C.**

When he kneeled down, he saw that a spot of brown paint had been knocked off, leaving a deep dent in the grille. He remembered there had been a bit of brown paint on the rear of the slide on Parks' pistol. He wondered if the gun could have caused the dent in the grille.

The gun, the bullet taken from Parks' body, the jammed cartridge case, and the grille were sent to the FBI Laboratory to be examined.

Laboratory experts found that the bullet which killed the former captain had been fired from Parks' own gun. But they also found some other interesting facts: the brown paint on the gun slide was similar in color and texture to the paint on the grille; the gun would fire when dropped on the rear part of the slide and the hammer; marks on the grille matched exactly similar marks made by the rear sight and knurling of the gun's hammer; and when the rear sight and hammer of the pistol were placed against the marks on the grille, the gun was pointing toward the spot where Parks had fallen.

Agents and police then reasoned that Parks had been working with the gun. In a sudden fit of temper, he had thrown it against the floor. It had struck the grille and fired. The cartridge case had jammed and the gun had skittered all the way across the living room, coming to rest against the wall. Parks had not lived long enough to tell his wife what had happened except that "the gun backfired."

The murder charge against Mrs. Parks was dropped.

The men in the FBI Laboratory never know from one day to the next what they will be asked to do. It may be a problem to be solved by chemistry, or physics, or electronics, or ballistics, or handwriting, or photography, or any of many other methods.

In one case the FBI was called on by the Navy to help find out what happened to a crack test pilot when his faster-than-sound jet plane mysteriously went out of control during an experimental flight. The pilot was putting the plane through tests in the thin, cold, upper atmosphere when something went wrong. The pilot was heard by radio to say: "Going to have to leave it!" Then his voice was lost in other sounds—and that was all.

Searchers found parts of the plane and the pilot's body. But there was no clue to what had happened in those final seconds. It was important to know why the pilot hadn't been able to get out of the cockpit.

A tape recording of the pilot's radio conversation with the ground personnel was sent to the Laboratory. The specialists set to work to filter the pilot's voice out of the babble of sound, part of it caused by the screaming dive of the plane. They were able to bring the pilot's voice out of all but the final moments of the dive.

The tape recording was transferred to a phonograph disc. Then by speeding up and slowing down the record at different places—and tinkering with the sound level—the pilot's voice began to break through the other sounds.

News that the pilot's last words had been filtered from the tape spread excitement through the Laboratory. Agents and technicians gathered to hear what it was that he had said. When the tape was played, they heard a voice calling desperately: "Can't bail out . . . can't . . . bail . . . out!"

The pilot had spoken only six words —but those six words were enough to point to a defect in the plane. Hearing the words meant that other planes in the future would be made safer for the men who flew them.

The work of Laboratory engineers has helped make the FBI perhaps the most mobile crime-fighting agency in the world. This is because of the Bureau's communications network which spreads by wire and radio across the nation.

The Headquarters in Washington, D. C., and the fifty-five field offices, are linked by telephone and teletype circuits. In addition the FBI has its own radio network by which control centers keep in touch with agents in automobiles or on foot—and agents can talk to each other even while trailing a suspect.

Hoover began planning the radio network when England was being bombed heavily by German bombers early in World War II. One of the biggest problems of the British was to keep telephone and telegraph lines repaired.

"We've got to face up to the problem," Hoover said. "Our own coastlines may become the targets for bombers and communications will be in danger. We can't afford to be immobilized in an emergency."

By the time the Japanese attacked Pearl Harbor, the FBI had the radio network in operation. It has been an important factor ever since in the Bureau's fight against crime, espionage, and subversion.

# 16. A Career in the FBI

Many boys dream of a career as an FBI agent. And the FBI's door is always open to those who can meet the tests that every agent must pass. Only a few are chosen each year. But those who make the grade can never say: "This is a dull, uninteresting life."

In return for loyalty and hard work, the FBI offers more than an exciting way of life. It offers among other things good pay, steady promotions for those who earn them, the satisfaction of serving the country, pride in organization, sickness and accident protection, family insurance, and a liberal pension plan.

Special agents in every state are always on the lookout in high schools, colleges, and universities for young men who they think would make good agents. The first requirements are:

1. They must be citizens of the United States.

2. They must be ready and willing to serve anywhere in the United States or Puerto Rico when ordered to do so.

3. They must possess the basic educational standards, which currently require that they be graduates of a state-accredited law school (not a correspondence school); or they must be college graduates who majored in accounting and have had at least three years experience in accounting or auditing.

4. They must be at least twenty-three years old but not more than forty years old.

5. They must be at least five-feet-seven in stocking feet; have 20/20 vision (corrected with glasses) and no color blindness; be able to hear normal conversation with each ear from a distance of fifteen feet; and be in top physical condition.

6. They must be able to drive a car and have a driver's license.

The young man who meets these tests can make an application to be an FBI agent. He is given oral and written examinations by one of the FBI's veteran special agents.

If the examinations go well, there still is no guarantee of appointment. After that, the FBI makes a thorough investigation of the applicant's background and his fitness to be an agent.

The man who gets through these stern tests has a good chance of getting an appointment on a one-year trial basis. Then he goes to Washington, D. C., to study the latest techniques in law enforcement, fingerprint identification, writing reports, crime detection, collecting evidence, and other things he must know to do his job properly.

The training period includes fourteen weeks of hard work at the FBI training facilities in Washington and at Quantico, Virginia, where the rookie is taught to use four basic weapons—pistol, submachine gun, shotgun, and rifle. He is taught how to take care of himself in a gun battle and how to take cover under fire. He learns the "fast draw" and how to shoot from a steady, crouching position. He learns to use weapons with either hand while standing, kneeling, sitting, or in a prone position—shooting at fixed and moving targets. He is taught physical defensive tactics and other tricks of close, rough fighting which he may one day have to use in order to protect himself and other agents.

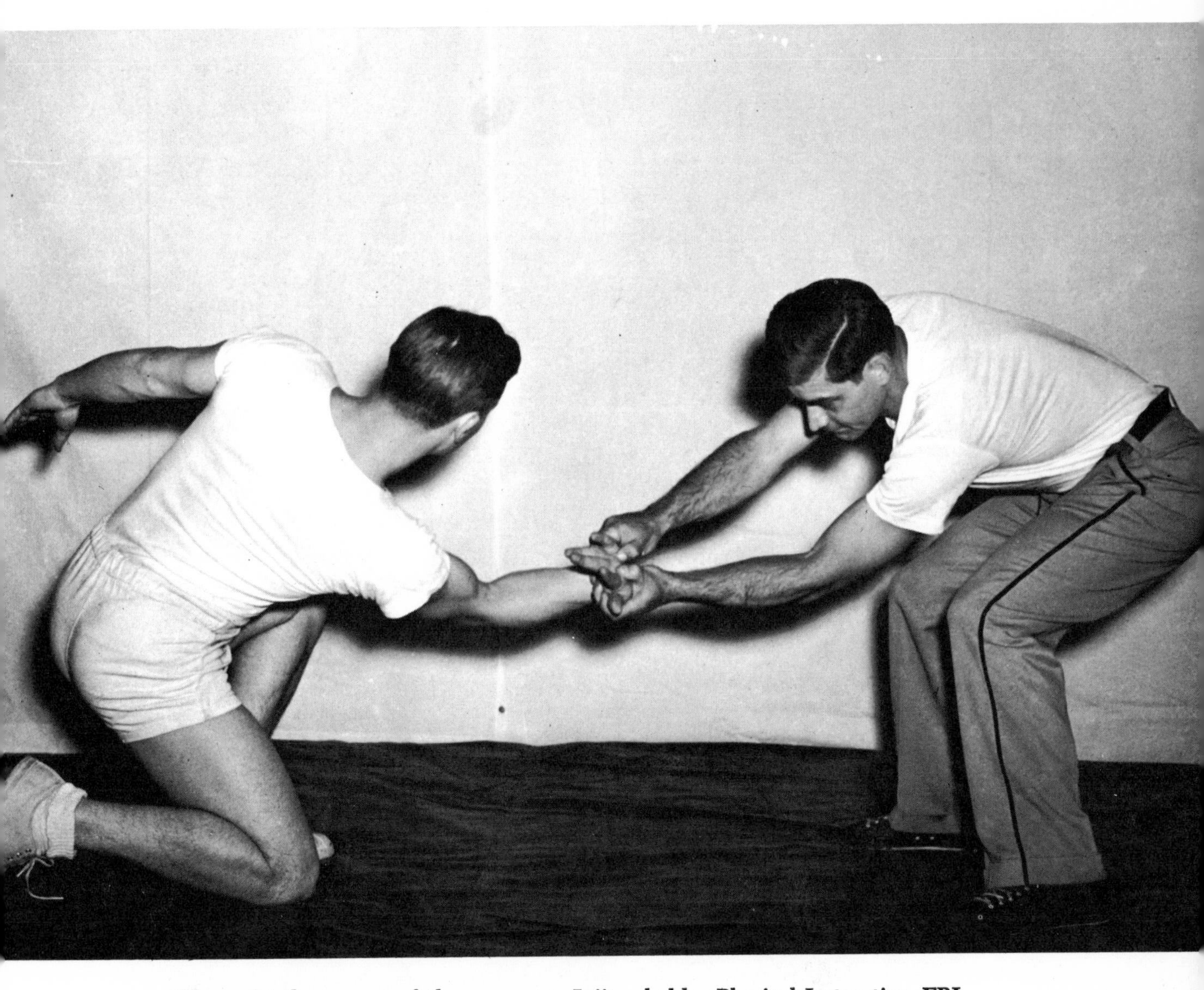

The wrist throw, one of the numerous Jujitsu holds. Physical Instruction, FBI, U.S. Department of Justice.

A special agent is shown kneeling in the double action firing position at the 25-yard line of the practical pistol course on the FBI range at Quantico, Virginia.

Among the first things a new agent learns is that there is no secret formula by which mysteries are solved or criminals tracked down. If there is any secret at all it lies in patience and hard work.

There has been no better example of this than the FBI's work in finding the kidnaper of one-month-old Peter Weinberger back in 1956. . . .

It was a warm Fourth of July and Mrs. Morris Weinberger thought it would be good for her baby to lie out on the patio of her home at Westbury, Long Island. So, after taking him for a stroll in his carriage, she decided to leave him on the patio while attending to other matters inside.

About 10 minutes later, Mrs. Weinberger came to the patio to see if Peter was all right. She was terrified to find the carriage empty. Where her son had lain was a handwritten note demanding that $2,000 be placed in a brown envelope and left next to a signpost not far from the Weinberger home.

Mrs. Weinberger called the Nassau County police. The FBI learned of the kidnaping at 8:40 P.M. and agents were sent to the Weinberger home to get the facts. At this time, there was no evidence that the child had been carried across state lines or that the kidnaper had used interstate communications such as a telephone or telegraph; so the matter was left to the local police.

The Weinbergers left the $2,000 in an envelope at the signpost as the ransom note demanded. But it was not picked up. The kidnaper then telephoned the Weinbergers; and another note from him, written on an order blank of a company dealing in window products, was found at Exit 28 of the Northern State Parkway immediately thereafter.

When Peter Weinberger had not been returned on the seventh day, the FBI entered the investigation under a special clause of the Federal Kidnap Statute. About the only clue the agents had was the handwriting on the ransom notes. This seemed to offer the best chance of finding the kidnaper.

A special headquarters was set up in Mineola, Long Island, and a squad of agents was assigned to the case. They were joined by handwriting experts sent from the Bureau in Washington, D. C.

The agents began what seemed to be an impossible task—to trace the kidnaper through his handwriting. They looked at the writing of tens of thousands of people in post office files, civil service files, police records, hospital records, automobile registrations, job applications, and business records.

Each time an agent came across handwriting that looked anything like the writing on the ransom note, it was sent to the experts at the special headquarters. The agents checked through nearly two million specimens of handwriting in their dogged search.

On August 22—forty-nine days after the kidnaping—an agent was in the Federal Court for the Eastern District of New York comparing handwriting in the court's records with a photographic copy of the ransom notes. He and another agent had just finished reviewing all of the available parole and probation records. They were preparing to leave when another group of records—which were out of the regular file—came to their attention. Among these was the probation file of Angelo John LaMarca.

LaMarca had been arrested two years earlier during a raid on an illicit still. He had been sentenced to ninety days in

Attention
I'm sorry this had to happen, but
I am in bad need of money, & couldn't
get it any other way.
Don't tell anyone or go to the Police
about this, because I am watching you
closely. I am scared stiff, & will kill
the baby, at your first wrong move.
Just put $2000 00/xxx (two thousand)
in small bills in a brown envelope, &
place it next to the sign post at the
corner of Albermarle Rd. & Park Ave.
at Exactly 10 o'clock tomorrow (Thursday)
morning. If everything goes smooth,
I will bring the baby back &
leave him on the same corner "Safe
& Happy" at exactly 12 noon.
No excuses, I cant wait!

Your baby sitter.

Copy of ransom note left by kidnaper of Peter Weinberger on July 4, 1956.

jail but the judge had suspended the sentence and placed him on probation for a year.

The handwriting of LaMarca looked very much like the handwriting on the ransom note. The agent immediately brought the file to the attention of handwriting experts at Mineola. They compared the writing in the file with the original notes.

"We've found our man," one of the experts said. "There's no doubt about it. The handwriting is the same."

The needle-in-the-haystack search was over. LaMarca confessed. In the garage where he worked as a mechanic, agents found a pad of order blanks similar to the one found at the exit to the Northern State Parkway.

The body of little Peter Weinberger was found the next day. Since the child had not been carried across a state line, the federal kidnaping law had not been violated. LaMarca was turned over to New York state authorities. As an aftermath of this case, Congress passed a law permitting the FBI to enter a kidnap case when the victim was missing for only twenty-four hours—rather than seven days.

Agents learn quickly that attention to detail is important. Associate Director Tolson was hammering on this point when he once said: "Precision is the cardinal virtue of an investigating agency. Many a criminal has been convicted, and many an innocent person absolved, because somebody took pains to be accurate about an 'unimportant little fact.' "

The new agent, even while in school, starts earning $7,290* a year. When he is sent to a field office, he can earn another $1,019* a year in overtime. Some of the older agents earn more than $15,000 yearly including their overtime. Those who are promoted to supervisory jobs are even better paid.

During his first few weeks in the field, the rookie works with more experienced agents. Then he is on his own. But his training in the classroom and on the firing range never ends until he retires.

At least once a year, inspectors from Headquarters check on each field office to be certain that they are operating efficiently. The work of the agents is under close watch at all times—a policy which Hoover has followed from the day he took over the Bureau.

Each agent must sign a register when he enters or leaves his office whether it's in New York, Washington, D. C., or any other office. Every two hours while on duty, he is expected to check by telephone with his office for any messages or emergency assignments—unless he is in a radio car. He reports where he is and what he is doing and this information is entered in a record. Thus the special agent in charge can check with the communications center at any time and know where all of his agents are.

The agent is expected to make a formal, written report at least each forty-five days on the cases on which he is working. If he lags behind in his reports, he is called in to explain. The field office that falls behind in its reports soon hears from Headquarters asking for an explanation.

Crime does not keep tidy office hours of 9:00 A.M. to 5:30 P.M. and so the FBI agent can not expect to be home with his family each evening at the same hour. He knows he may be called on suddenly

* These figures will increase in January, 1964.

**Finish of hip throw used to counter a right-hand blow. Physical Instruction, FBI, U.S. Department of Justice.**

to help investigate an airplane crash, a kidnaping, a bank robbery, or an espionage case which could take him from home for days or weeks.

This kind of life—where the men live with danger—has forged a "one for all and all for one" spirit within the FBI that is one of its strengths. Bureau files are filled with cases in which the FBI looked out for its own as it did when Special Agents W. Carter Baum and Sam Cowley were killed in gun battles in the 1930s. Both their widows came to work for the FBI and remained as long as they wished. In illnesses or emergencies, members of the "family" look after one another.

The chances are that the man who becomes an FBI agent will stay on to make a career. Among the Bureau's 6,000 agents, a total of nearly 80 per cent have been with the FBI for ten years or more —and over 30 per cent have served for more than twenty years.

FBI employees are not under civil service, but they are entitled to the same benefits and privileges received by other government employees—with a little more added.

The Bureau has no women agents but many of its employees are women working as typists, clerks, technicians, and stenographers. Young girls arriving in Washington, D. C., for the first time are told where they can rent rooms in approved homes, where to find churches, and the best places for recreation.

"If there is anything bothering you or anything we can do to help," they are told, "all you have to do is call the Bureau. Somebody is there day and night just for that purpose."

The FBI Recreation Association makes sure there is no reason for any employee to be lonely. It organizes dances, tours, moonlight excursions, picnics, camp shows, and sports activities—with clubs for those who like travel, flying, coin collecting, pistol shooting, and other special hobbies.

Among other benefits open to FBI employees are:

*Federal Employees Group Life Insurance*—Employees may buy term life insurance at a cost of $6.50 per year per $1,000 of coverage. A new agent earning $7,290* a year is entitled to $8,000 of insurance, and in all cases insurance may be bought in the amount of the nearest thousand dollars above the annual salary. The insurance pays double for any type of accidental death.

*Special Agents' Insurance Fund*—Available only to the FBI agents. It provides in addition to the Federal Employees Group Insurance $10,000 payment in case of death from any cause. Payments are made by the agents in the form of ten-dollar assessments whenever the reserve fund requires such payment. Since November, 1943, the assessment has averaged less than $17 a year.

A basic accident policy offers protection against accidental death, permanent total disability, and loss of an arm, leg, etc. It may be bought in any amount from $10,000 to $200,000 for eighty-five cents per thousand and includes options for medical expenses and payments while away from work because of an accident.

*Sick Leave*—Earned at the rate of thirteen working days a year. There is

* In January, 1964, the starting salary for newly appointed FBI Agents will increase from $7,290 to $7,690 pursuant to Public Law 793 of the 87th Congress.

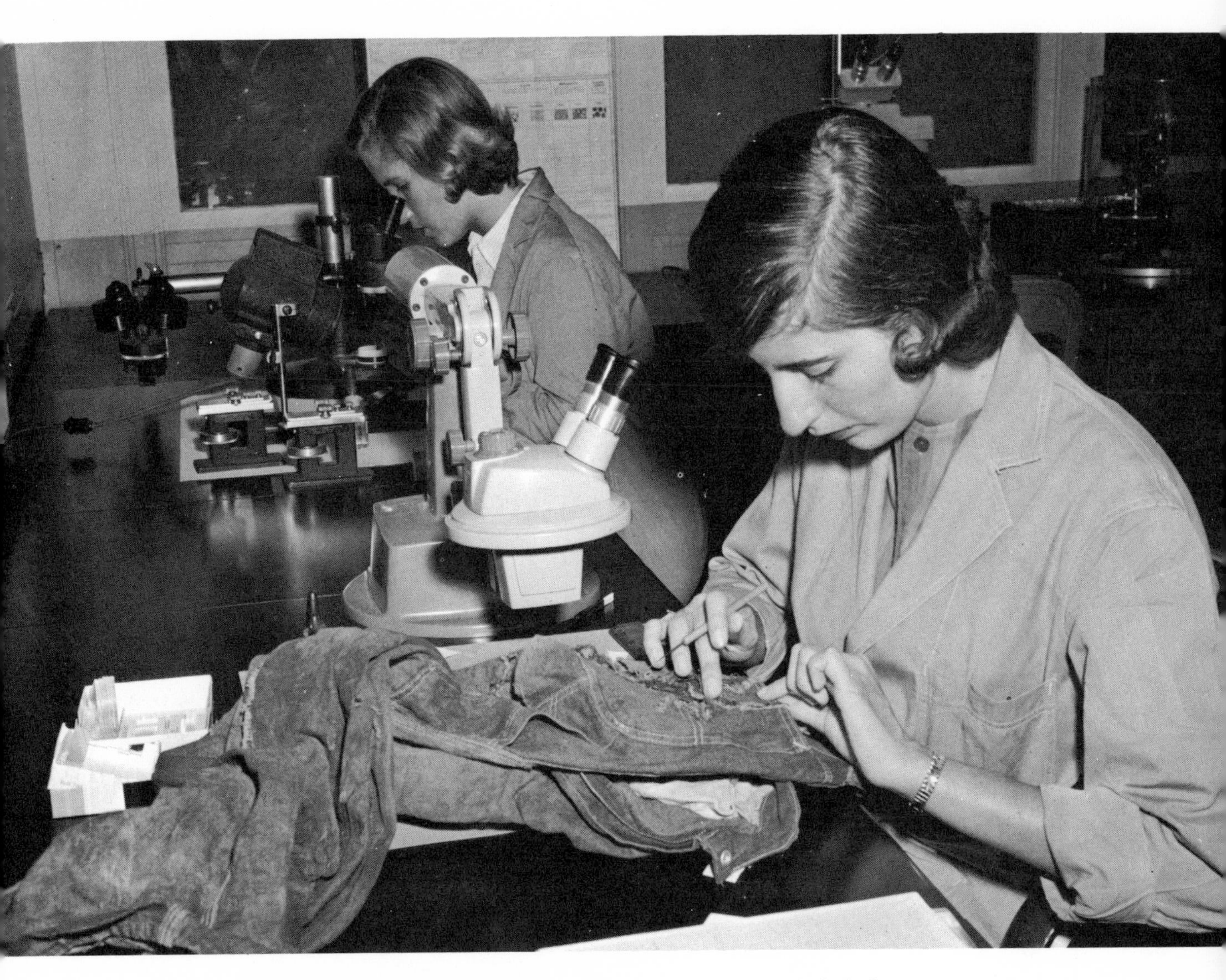

A laboratory technician is shown identifying a piece of cloth from a crime scene with a torn area in the trousers of a suspect, FBI Laboratory, Washington, D.C.

**A special agent firing double action in the hip level position from the 7-yard line of the practical pistol course on the FBI range at Quantico, Virginia.**

**FBI pistol range at the United States Marine Corps Base at Quantico, Virginia. Special agents are shown point shooting at 25 yards at silhouette targets.**

no limit on the number of days that may be accumulated, and many employees have over 200 days of sick leave to their credit.

*Annual Leave*—Those with fewer than three years of service are entitled to thirteen working days leave each year. Those with three years but less than fifteen years of service are entitled to twenty working days leave; and those with fifteen or more years in service are entitled to twenty-six working days.

*Federal Employees Health Benefits Program*—All eligible employees may join in an approved plan with the government paying part of the cost and the employee paying the balance through a payroll deduction. The FBI's plan is called the Special Agents Mutual Benefit Association (Samba). In addition to providing hospitalization and surgical benefits (including $30,000 major medical benefits), membership in Samba includes $2,000 life insurance with other benefits optional.

*Compensation*—All employees are covered by the Federal Employees' Compensation Act. It entitles them to medical, hospital, and loss-of-pay benefits in case injuries are suffered in performance of official duties.

*Retirement and Survivorship Benefits*—An agent may retire at age fifty after twenty years of service as an agent. If this represents his total federal service, he would receive 40 per cent of the average annual salary he was paid during the top five consecutive years of his career. At the end of forty years, the maximum retirement pay is 80 per cent.

There are survivor benefits for the widow and children under eighteen of an employee who has had at least five years of civilian service. The cost of all retirement benefits is 6½ per cent of the employee's salary.

**The FBI rifle range at the United States Marine Corps Base at Quantico, Virginia. Twenty-four special agents are firing in a kneeling position at 200 yards.**

As an example of the benefits paid to the survivors of an agent who was killed in an automobile accident in line of duty, the agent's widow received $84,-703.83 in lump sum benefits:

|  |  |
|---|---|
| Federal Employees Group Life Insurance (double indemnity) | $26,000.00 |
| Special Agents' Insurance Fund | 10,000.00 |
| Special Agents Mutual Benefit Association (double indemnity) | 12,000.00 |
| Special Accident and Travel Insurance | 20,000.00 |
| Salary and vacation pay due | 5,685.58 |
| Funeral expenses paid by Bureau of Employees' Compensation | 800.00 |
| Civil Service Retirement Fund | 10,218.25 |
| Total | $84,703.83 |

In addition, under the Federal Employees' Compensation Act, the widow and her two children will receive payments of $6,300 a year as long as they are eligible.

It is only fair to say that a career in the FBI is not for those who want an easy, sheltered life—just as the Marine Corps is not a place for anyone who is not ready to fight when called to do so by his country.

There is always danger in hunting criminals, spies, and subversives. The hours can be long and rugged. The code of conduct is stern and demands more than some are willing to give.

But being an FBI agent also has its rewards, which are many. Not the least of these is the respect which the FBI under J. Edgar Hoover has earned the hard way in almost forty years of fighting for decent law enforcement and for the security of the nation.

# Index